Wild about Weeds

Published in 2019 by
Laurence King Publishing
361–373 City Road
London EC1V 1LR
United Kingdom
T + 44 (0)20 7841 6900
enquiries@laurenceking.com
www.laurenceking.com

A catalog record for this book is available from
the British Library.

ISBN 978-1-78627-556-1

Commissioning editor: Camilla Morton
Editors: Deborah Hercun, Melissa Danny
Designer: Masumi Briozzo
Picture researcher: Kendra Wilson

Printed in China

Laurence King Publishing is committed to ethical and sustainable
production. We are proud participants in The Book Chain Project®
bookchainproject.com

Front cover: Jim Powell (Sarah Price garden, RHS Chelsea
Flower Show)
Back cover: David Dixon/Gap Photos
Dedicated to Topher

Wild about Weeds

Garden Design with Rebel Plants

Jack Wallington

Laurence King Publishing

Contents

Opposite: *Cirsium vulgare* (thistle) seed heads,
Cosmos, and *Urtica dioica*.

Introduction

Previous page: *Papaver rhoeas, Ruta chalepensis, Dorycnium pentaphyllum, Santolina rosmarinifolia, Papaver dubium* ssp. *lecoqii albiflorum, Papaver somniferum* "Lauren's Grape," *Euphorbia rigida, Senecio mandraliscae.* Opposite: *Digitalis purpurea, Urtica dioica, Ranunculus acris,* and *Urtica dioica.*

Looking for the right place

People often say to me, "If only this plant would grow as well as my weeds." It strikes me as an interesting statement, because if one plant is growing happily and the other not, perhaps the plants are telling us something.

I've always loved weeds. They sneak into our gardens hoping to flower before we notice. A garden without weeds is a soulless, lifeless thing. But, more than that, the last weed you pulled out may have been destined to transform your garden in the most beautiful and unpredictable ways.

Driving around New Zealand I've seen thousands of lupins growing as weeds in people's gardens, but also along roadsides as an introduced invasive. In the wild this is a problem for native plants and wildlife, but in gardens there is no denying their towering beauty. In North America, native Pennisetum grass can be found as a weed along highways. Japan cultivates moss to the point the rest of the world envies its use, yet elsewhere we blast it from the face of the Earth with a jet washer.

Weeds have a problem the world over. When we lose control of a plant, its presence feels suffocating and our reaction is to get rid of it entirely. However, if we stop for a moment to appreciate weedy plants, without the negative propaganda, we find attractive, often pretty, things. By taking time to understand weeds better, we can enjoy the beauty of them in gardens while preventing them from escaping into the wild.

Years ago, on my community garden in London, a tiny weed appeared growing among my beans. Intrigue, empathy—whatever the reason—I left that weed to see what it would become. A year later I'd forgotten about it entirely, itself buried beneath other weeds. Then, one dusk, there it was, a glowing white spire with the golden sun setting behind it: *Digitalis purpurea* subsp. *albiflora*, the less common form of Europe's native foxglove (see p.21), igniting a weedy epiphany. What if these weeds, seen as problem plants to be evicted, are actually creating easy beauty if we bother to stop to look?

I'd already been leaving in my designs a few weeds that I liked: *Anagallis arvensis* (see p.128) with its gorgeous, dusty orange flowers; *Oxalis corniculata* var. *atropurpurea* (see p.134)—against the advice

of many gardeners—I loved for its purple-brown, heart-shaped leaves with perfect edges, which show off its bright yellow flower; *Euphorbia helioscopia*, with acid-green flowers among the purple of my cabbages. They didn't seem to be causing the problems people said they would, and I liked the look of them. That's it, I thought, they're staying.

More than a plant

Since childhood I've felt a connection with weeds. Behind our family's cottage garden in Buckinghamshire, I used to run through forests of *Heracleum mantegazzianum* (I understood its sap was dangerous; see p.106), I swung from jungle vines of *Clematis vitalba*, and I stomped over *Hedera helix* (see p.132). When I was about seven, I remember feeding our dandelions with fertilizer to grow bigger flowers.

Weeds were the first flowers I knew, they are probably the first flowers anyone knows—the little daisy and buttercup in the lawn. Blowing dandelion puffballs. In fact, ask most people to name flowers and I'm sure these will come up more than many garden varieties.

While many people get frustrated with weeds in gardens, I've grown increasingly fond of them. They're beautiful, they're part of the natural world, attracting bees and butterflies, and they're connected to our lives. Part of me likes them because they're so familiar. Familiarity provides a link, a friend, an emotional or nostalgic connection.

Another part of me—the rebellious, weed-like part!—likes weeds purely because other people tell me not to.

Weeds enhancing design

These days, as a professional garden designer and horticulturist, I actively incorporate weeds into my own garden and into designs for clients. Not all weeds are ugly, uncontrollable brutes. Many, including those I've selected for this book, are beautiful plants with colorful flowers and a habit that suits modern garden style.

As I've explored and discussed the world of weeds with people, I've found that everyone has at least one weed that they let off the hook, one they leave in their garden. Often it fills a gap where nothing else grows, it has a personal connection, or it feels right for the place.

Many gardeners I work with grow more than one weed in their clients' gardens, understanding the weed's beauty, using just enough control to stop them dominating. Some have even taken weeds to the height of horticultural excellence, including weeds in gold-medal-winning designs at the world-famous Chelsea Flower Show.

Perhaps some plants become so ubiquitous we start to dislike them, drawn instead to something shiny and new. I'm as guilty of this as anyone, but I also like to look at familiar plants with fresh eyes. There's something comforting about the familiar and there's always a different, imaginative way to present them to make them feel new.

This book explores this much-ridiculed and ripped-out group of plants and argues that through understanding weeds, not only will we become better gardeners, but our gardens will become the magical, beautiful spaces we dream of.

Taming the weedy wildflower

Somewhere there's an unspoken scale that ranks plants from "weed" to "wildflower" to "ornamental." At one end sits *Fallopia japonica* (see p.28) and, at the other, *Hyacinthoides non-scripta* (see p.22), and *Rosa canina* (see p.164) sit in the middle feeling confused.

No one has ever published the rules of this scale and it seems to change according to who's talking. One person's weedy *Meconopsis cambrica* (see p.100) is another's garden ornamental; still others will swear it's a wildflower. Frankly, the *Meconopsis cambrica* is both all and none of these things.

It seems strange to me that *Geranium robertianum* (see p.94) is considered a weed, while *Myosotis sylvatica* (see p.22) isn't. Or that someone who loves the look of daisies should be made to feel bad about them growing in their lawn. Why do lawns always have to be green? If I can ever afford a lawn of my own, it will be the weediest, most colorful lawn ever to be walked on. Some weeds, like *Oenothera biennis* (see p.72) were introduced as garden plants. A plant is a plant and if you like it, you should grow it no matter what anyone else thinks or what label it's been given. Labels are annoying. They're often someone else's opinion telling us what we should think. "Weed" being a good example—it is merely a broad and negative term associated with any plant that pops up where we weren't expecting it. The label is a lie.

What is a weed?

The standard definition of a weed is "a plant in the wrong place," which seems to make sense on the face of it, but it doesn't get to the heart of the issue. Ask a farmer what a weed is and he or she will tell you it's a plant that ruins crops or harms livestock. Conservationists

(I include myself) would say weeds are invasive plants that humans (usually) have introduced and that interfere with natural ecosystems. Gardeners on the other hand generally tell me a weed is a hair-rippingly annoying plant that simply will not go away.

In the wrong place, certainly, but each reason for being so is very different. We, as gardeners, are in charge of what does and doesn't grow in our gardens. Rightly so. Gardens are personal spaces where humanity and nature collide in a beautiful collaboration. Striking the balance between designed and natural is the challenge only humans as a species are capable of meeting.

Even if we like the look of a plant, if it persists and spreads easily to the point it's difficult to control, we probably get frustrated with it and it becomes a weed. But ultimately only you can decide if a plant is a weed in your eyes. Don't let other people define what you can or can't like—it's your garden and only you can say what should and shouldn't have a place in it.

For the purpose of this book, I have defined a garden weed as "a plant that reproduces seemingly uncontrollably." From the plants that fit into this definition, I have then divided them into the good, the bad, and the unappreciated. The good weeds have made it into enough hearts to be called wildflowers or even "garden worthy," the bad are those that I felt really are more uncontrollable than worthwhile and, to my eye (if you like them that's fine!), are not easy to design with. The unappreciated are that middle ground, the plants I believe have unfairly been stamped as bad, but should be in the good category. I'm sticking up for the unappreciated weeds and they form the bulk of this book.

The sign of a good gardener

Reassuringly, I'm not alone. One look at the best-designed gardens recently and you'll spot a weed used as a key garden plant. Why? Some of today's most experienced gardeners and designers—who have contributed interviews to this book—are not just taking out, but also adding weeds into their garden beds and pots. It's a modern approach made possible through improved plant knowledge, and the results can be exquisite.

Many show gardens at the Chelsea Flower Show that included weeds have won gold medals. Garden designer James Basson's "Maltese Quarry" garden incorporated many plants from Malta that people would consider weeds. The design was named Best in Show in 2017.

Sprinkling flowering weeds into the mixture with ornamentals always seems to pay off with judges and the crowds. People don't always immediately realize they're looking at familiar weeds, the new context casting a different light on them. Many gardeners who do spot them are overjoyed, perhaps because they've harbored a love for these colorful miscreants, but never before been given such open permission to celebrate them.

Of course, there are always a few who can't see past the label of "it's a weed."

Weeds aren't always messy

In gardens, weeds are those unplanned plants that pop up to thwart our careful, considered design efforts. They add color we didn't want, grow where we wanted a bit of breathing space, give shape that throws off our intended balance. I could argue that it's not the weed's fault that we hatched a plan without it, but I know all too well those plants are breaking our rules, those little rebels. And while they may well be rebelling against our tyranny of the garden, perhaps we should listen to what these rebels have to say.

Through improved understanding of the nature of weeds and looking at ways to design gardens that aren't static, this book will show you how to incorporate weeds beautifully (and tidily) into designed spaces, even formal or clean-cut designs. For example, for each featured weed we'll look at allocating specific spots in which that weed can grow, using its life cycle to restrict its spread. Weeds are rebel plants. Their agenda doesn't always fit ours, sometimes it can be better.

Sustainable and wildlife-friendly

Weeds will grow where it suits them best, you don't need to fight against the conditions by changing the soil pH, watering regularly or adding fertilizer. This can mean less work for you (an important point to remember) and it also puts less pressure on the environment.

Weeds are loved by wildlife, too—for nectar, shelter, nibbling on. Long flowering periods help. It seems a shame to prevent this because we've been told a plant is a weed. Levels of benefit for wildlife will depend on the particular species, as well as where it's growing in the world. Sometimes a weed will have more insects feeding off it in its native country than where humans have introduced it, but not always—sometimes the opposite is true; there are no general rules.

None of this needs to come before design: everyone can find a weed for their design that ticks the eco-friendly boxes without resorting to scruffy areas of unmanaged grass and bug hotels made from junk. Highly formal designs can be as wildlife-friendly as naturalistic ones, and weeds can be as tidy and formal as the most trimmed and pruned of ornamental flowers.

Above: *Daucus carota* used in a smart and stylish structured garden bed.

Be a rebel

This book is for adventurous, future-thinking gardeners. For people who like to question rules and the so-called "correct way of doing things." It is for people tired of weeding the garden; for those who struggle to grow particular plants and for those wanting easy beauty that's wildlife-friendly and ecologically responsible. This book explains why and how some weeds can enhance your garden, improve water-management, and reduce maintenance and cost while bringing you closer to nature. All within the setting of contemporary, designed outdoor spaces.

My hope is that you find at least one weed that you love, a fellow garden rebel in a world of labels we didn't invent.

Designing with Rebel Plants

Opposite: *Leucanthemum vulgare,*
Plantago lanceolata, and *Ranunculus acris*
beneath *Cornus kousa* "Milky Way."

Designing with weeds is no different in principle to designing with any other plants. I've used *Anthriscus sylvestris* (see p.104) and *Cenolophium denudatum* in both modern and traditional garden bed designs; *Fumaria officinalis* (see p.70) in tropical raised beds alongside banana plants; and even *Bellis perennis* (see p.118) in window boxes. However, weeds provide us with a unique opportunity to use their tendency to spread to create designs that become more dynamic over time.

Keep things simple

A garden designed using only weeds is perfectly possible, but in fact it makes more sense to use one or two weeds alongside other ornamentals. These could be weeds you introduce into your garden, or problem weeds you already have and can't get rid of. We all know that weeds on the loose need care and attention, so limiting the types of weed included in a design to just a few keeps things manageable.

Look more closely at weeds

Spend some quality time with the weeds in your area, get to know them better and you're already halfway to designing with them. Look for a weed in perfect health—as you would expect any garden plant to be. Reassess it. What are its flowers like? What shapes are the leaves? Is it growing sporadically around the area or forming a close-knit group? Is it in sun or shade, dry or damp soil? If you were to pair it with another plant in your garden, which would it be?

Now, try picking the flowers of a number of weeds and ornamental plants that you think might look good together. Arrange them loosely in a vase of water where you can see the flowers close up.

A weed in the right place

It might seem odd to use the well-known term "right plant, right place" when a weed is a plant in the wrong place, but the same rules apply. Day to day, we don't tend to treat weeds well—is it any wonder, then, that we so often see only the worst in them. Choose weeds that will grow happily in the conditions they like to make sure they look their best at all times (the weed entries in the book will help you). For example, grow *Lamium album* (see p.98) in too sunny a spot and it will develop crispy, burnt leaves that look tatty; in shade, though, it produces lush green growth and the purest white flowers. Healthy, happy weeds, like all plants, look better.

Simply observing a weed's natural habitat can tell you all you need to know about what it likes. However, sometimes it is better to put the right weed in the wrong place—after all, planting in less favorable conditions can be just what that weed (or your garden) needs to slow its spread. *Eutrochium maculatum* is a good example: drier soils will tame this damp-loving plant enough to make it manageable.

Keeping weeds in tip-top condition

Weeds left to their own devices can look messy. It's not really their fault, it's ours. Ornamental plants have the luxury of being primped, pruned, fed and deadheaded, giving them an unfair advantage.

Weeds in the right location are unlikely ever to need fertilizing, but they do need some attention from time to time. In very hot, summer months, even weeds could do with the occasional water to prevent their leaves crisping up under intense sun or drying winds.

Weeds as the foundation of a design

One of the reasons people dislike weeds is because they don't fit our plans—they're the wrong color, shape, or style. Unfortunately for us, when a weed has chosen our garden as the place to kick off its shoes and set up camp, it's unlikely to leave without a fight.

A new approach to this effort is to start with the weed. What color and size is it? What ornamental plants would go with it? Approaching a garden design with a weed as the wash to your canvas may sound like madness, but it makes for long-term sense. Design a garden to work with that weed and it will always feel an easygoing part of the plan.

For example, I worked on a prairie design in a place where the ground was overrun with *Oxalis corniculata* var. *atropurpurea* (see p.134) with its dusky, purple-brown leaves, and *Anagallis arvensis* (see p.128) with dusky, orange flowers. Instead of starting a war I knew I could never win, I created the entire prairie design from the weeds up.

I incorporated larger ornamental prairie plants with dusky orange and purple flowers to match the weeds. I included *Kniphofia* "Tawny King," *Dierama pulcherrimum* "Blackbird," and the bronze of grasses *Nassella tenuissima* and *Calamagrostis brachytricha*. White flowers from *Achillea millefolium*, so often found in lawns, lifted the color palette.

The result was a beautiful prairie overrun with very low, ground-cover weeds that added to the underlying design canvas without affecting the growth of the bigger plants. The weeds formed such a tight ground cover they stopped unwanted weeds getting in.

Of course, there's nothing to stop you introducing weeds that you don't already have. I introduced *Linaria purpurea* (see p.60) into our garden because it matches our color palette and I like its tall, slender flower spires and leaves. I'd seen it growing nearby, which added to the sense of place, so collected some seeds and scattered them around. So far it's decided to grow only in the pot of my fig tree.

Gardens that change over time

Like all plants, weeds suit formal and traditional garden layouts. However, many are particularly suited to the popular, naturalistic style of garden, in which plants are more blended; where they grow and mingle into one another rather than sitting in blocks or groups.

In addition to choosing where a weed should grow, the beauty of rebellious plants is their potential to move around. A plant's ability to produce offspring in other parts of a garden, so often deemed a negative trait, in fact is an opportunity.

In many ways using weeds in gardens is no different to using any plant that likes to spread. *Aquilegia vulgaris* is a common cottage plant that behaves quite weedily, self-seeding everywhere in the right conditions. The key to this type of plant is to be ready for mischief and to put in place boundaries that limit spread.

We must stop thinking of a plant popping up in the middle of a carefully planned combination as a problem. Unexpected, yes, but is it really a bad thing? It may be an improvement, especially if you planned your design using that color. Instead of planning every plant position in a garden like pieces of a puzzle, we should try to see plants (all plants, weeds, and ornamentals alike) as ingredients in a tasty salad. Mix together the right quantities and, even though you can't control the presentation, the colors and shapes just look right.

Many gardens I visit have lots of planned structure, but allow a few weeds or other self-seeders, such as *Meconopsis cambrica* (see p.100), to pop up where they want. Although we have the least control over these plants, they actually bring the most cohesion to a garden. Plants that reproduce and spread will change a garden over time, but that doesn't mean the garden has to be messy. Planned gardens can be in constant flux and yet look smart and stylish.

In reality you're likely to plant a combination of 70–90 percent static and well-behaved plants with only 10–30 percent rebels. If you

yourself are feeling particularly rebellious, though, go with 100 percent weeds and you will effectively have a wonderful garden meadow.

Combining weeds for your design

Think about the following factors when choosing weeds and other plants for your design.

Color: This is critical for making or breaking a palette: and although there are no set rules (the most important thing is to choose a palette that works for you), too chaotic can become garish. Weeds come in the same variety of colors as ornamental plants, although the palette is slightly more limited owing to a lack of bred cultivars. Every design has a core of complementary colors (which are closest to each other on the color wheel and similar pigments), making a design feel unified.

Alone though, complementary colors can make a design feel flat, so introducing one or more contrasting colors helps to bring a design to life; to make it pop. Pastel colors can feel calmer and more relaxing; bold, vibrant colors, more exciting and lively. You can combine the two, but do so with care, because you don't want things to start to look odd. Think about tone and shade: for example, a deep magenta rose against lavender blue works well. Think about leaves, too—not all leaves are green. And, anyway there are many different shades of green from bright and fresh lime, to rich dark greens and even silvery blue. I very rarely include many more than four colors in the same garden bed (including green), but I will allow any number of shades.

Flowering months and longevity: Knowing when a weed flowers and how long for is critical to planning—it helps coordinate plants to flower together. For example, daffodils flower in spring and *Oenothera biennis* (see p.72) flowers in summer—they will never flower at the same time. Knowing when a weed flowers also allows you to pair a long-flowered weed with two or more short-flowered ones for different displays in the same year. For example, *Hirschfeldia incana* (see p.56) flowers from spring into fall, making a great backdrop to larger, showy flowers, such as alliums and later lilies, which have a shorter flowering window.

Height and width: Think about the size of your plants when you're deciding where to place them. Taller plants, such as *Dipsacus fullonum* (see p.66) and *Oenothera biennis* (see p.72) are generally planted at the backs of garden beds, while smaller plants, such as *Geranium robertianum* (see p.94) and *Meconopsis cambrica* (see p.100) are planted at the front, so that all the plants receive enough light and we can see them all. Be creative, though, because there are exceptions. Tall, slender plants, such as *Euphorbia lathyris* (see p.92) and *Solidago rigida*, allow light to pass through them easily and are sometimes worth bringing forward in a garden bed to create variety in heights, making the design more interesting with nooks and crannies to peer around.

Shape and form: Plants with contrasting shape and form help to add extra layers of interest. For example, *Achillea millefolium* and *Anthriscus sylvestris* (see p.104) have flat umbels of flowers held upright. Growing them with plants that have differently shaped flowers helps to improve the look. A very attractive shady combination might be *Anthriscus sylvestris* next to the whorls of flowers of shorter *Lamium album* (see p.98), and then *Digitalis purpurea* subsp. *albiflora* (see p.21), with its tall, slender spires.

Foliage: Don't forget to look at the leaves! Are they large and round, long and thin, shiny or matte. Leaves are as important as flowers, sometimes more so, as they last longer.

Texture: Think about the overall texture that the plant creates. For example, *Geranium robertianum* (see p.94), *Fumaria officinalis* (see p.70), *Eschscholzia californica* (see p.68) and *Hirschfeldia incana* (see p.56) are all highly textured plants making them good for contrasting with plants that have a more solid leaf.

Changes during growth: Something many people don't consider is how a plant changes as it grows. Ferns for example, have an incredible moment when their fronds unfurl in spring, but they are then static for most of the remainder of the year. *Euphorbia lathyris* (see p.92) spends the first year as a very geometric foliage plant. In its second year, though, it takes on a dramatically larger, more colorful form. Both forms are visually striking, but for very different reasons.

Root structure: Although we don't see the roots of the plant, their form and structure are important considerations when you're designing a garden. We talk about this more on pages 45–6.

The dead plant: Does the weed die back in winter and, if so, does it hold its shape? *Dipsacus fullonum* (see p.66) and *Centaurea nigra* (see p.80) are good examples of weeds that die back but hold their structure over winter. The golden brown and darker seed heads make a great winter silhouette, especially in the low winter sun or when covered in frost.

A final word of caution

This book has been written for a global audience with the aim to offer advice on growing weeds that you like in your garden, wherever in the world you might be. However, all plants, not just weeds, behave differently in different environments. What can be a well-behaved plant in one location may be invasive in another. This variation between regions and countries is so wide-ranging that one book

Above: *Ipomoea* growing unrestricted in Porto, Portugal.

can't cover everything! I have, however, of the weeds included here, highlighted those that might be a problem in the US. Some of the plants listed may not be appropriate in some states so it is always best to check first with your local authority.

Lythrum salicaria (see p.108) is a good example. In Europe, it is considered an attractive wildflower and (weedy) garden plant, whereas in the wild areas on the east coast of North America it is a bigger problem and authorities request that residents don't grow it. Please always check your own local laws before planting anything, and, of course, be sure you really understand how to grow and control the plant in your climate and soil conditions before introducing it.

As well as giving advice on how to plant weeds, I've also explained how to control and eradicate them—making this book useful for identifying and then removing weeds already in your garden that are noxious.

A Brief History of Garden Weeds

What came first—the weed or the garden?

A weed's ability to quickly colonize bare ground hasn't happened by accident. Most weeds evolved their "live fast, reproduce lots" behavior across many hundreds of thousands of years. Before humans began working the earth, avalanche, fire, and animal activity disturbed the soil, opening up gaps that gave space for opportunistic weeds to germinate. At the same time animals roaming the Earth ate seeds, which, once excreted in feces, rapidly germinated. The planet's dense coverage of woodland, scrub, and grasslands, meanwhile, kept these plants in check.

In the Neolithic era, about 12,000 years ago, greedy plants will have felt they'd won the lottery when humans learned to work on the land. Weeds had a field day—literally. In the first steps toward formal agriculture, humans cleared vast areas to grow crops—inevitably becoming the first salient beings to contend with weeds. Over the millennia that followed, as we felled more forests and created more fields, the weedy situation escalated.

There is evidence to suggest that many weed species have adapted to coexist with human activity, making them better able to exploit land around us. Some weeds have increased both the speed at which they reproduce and the quantity of seed they produce. A matter of natural selection, those plants that happen to produce more seed and produce it faster than their relatives will eventually outcompete and become the dominant strain.

If there is one weed in your garden that is particularly annoying, it's probably living with humans that helped it to evolve and become even more annoying. Every time you remove or dig out weeds, the strongest will still survive and regrow, contributing further to this "weedvolution." It's not the weed's fault it's weedy, it's yours.

The first weeds

Fossils tell us that weeds existed millions of years ago, but fossils are the only early records we have, so we will never know exactly when weeds first evolved. We do know, however, that some of the first successful plant groups were the spore-producing field horsetails and ferns, their descendants being weedy around gardens today.

In 2015, ecology professor Sergei Volis published a research article that gave evidence of weeds—including *Fumaria densiflora* (closely related to *Fumaria officinalis* on page 70) and *Silybum marianum*—used as human food in a 23,000-year-old human camp on the shores of the Sea of Galilee, Israel. The camp comes from our hunter-gatherer era, long before the time when humans began actually cultivating plants as food.

Weeds and art

Evidence of the human veneration of weeds comes from paintings and murals dating as far back as the time of ancient Egypt, with images of a species of *Convolvulus* (a bindweed) apparently used as a symbol of respect or mourning.

Through the ages, alongside paintings of cultivated flowers, such as tulips and roses, weeds (dandelions and daisies among them) appear regularly, even in medieval sculpture and carvings. Victorians, known

Opposite: *Papaver rhoeas* (common poppy).
Above: Morris & Co. drew inspiration from weeds like *Trifolium pratense* (red clover).

for their particular love and fascination of the natural world, were perhaps ahead of their time. Weeds regularly appeared in the most popular Victorian fashions and in designer patterns for wallpapers and upholstery fabric. It's worth popping to your nearest art gallery or museum to see how many weeds you can spot in art from across the centuries.

Today, contemporary art doesn't forget the humble weed: graffiti and household furnishings still use weeds—as symbols of nostalgia or wilderness, perhaps; and even possibly as a nod to rebelliousness.

Weeds for wellbeing

Although the earliest gardens on record tended primarily to be for produce, they did also serve as a place of rest and reflection. In the fifteenth century, for example, monks at Mount Grace's Carthusian Priory in North Yorkshire used their private garden "cells" as a means to aid mental wellbeing. For medieval Christians, in particular, a garden provided a link to God and the Garden of Eden; as did paradise gardens for Muslims.

In medieval times gardens provided vegetables, fruit, and herbs to eat, but also plants for medicinal use. Among them were weeds we know today: *Taraxacum officinale*, *Centranthus ruber* (see p.120), *Achillea millefolium*, and many others. *Achillea*, for example, was thought to help ease the pain of headaches and serious wounds. If our ancestors could grow, manage, and use these plants both for food and medicine, and indeed as ornamental additions to their gardens, why can't we?

Weeds of farmland

Rebel plants are the biggest adversary to farming. Weeds such as *Centaurea cyanus* and *Papaver rhoeas* grow on bare, disturbed ground—when farmers turn their fields, they provide the largest expanses of land on which weeds can thrive. Problems arise when weeds compete with crops for sun, water, and nutrients, affecting the harvest.

For farmers, the worst event of all is when a weed is mixed up with a crop, rendering the crop unusable and unsellable. Some wild grasses have evolved alongside human attempts to eradicate them, gradually mimicking crops, such as wheat and rice, through selection. We try to weed it out, but inevitably miss the weeds that look most like the crop. Over centuries, those clever weeds continually aim to out-do us, becoming more and more similar in appearance to the plants we're trying to cultivate, increasing the weed's chances of survival and their ability to proliferate.

But it's not just crop farmers who suffer from the nuisance of weeds. Some weeds are poisonous to livestock. Usually animals are smart

Above: *Plantago lanceolata*.

enough to avoid plants that harm them—you may reasonably expect to see a field chomped to the ground except for *Jacobaea vulgaris* (see p.58) standing above the short grass. However, where livelihood and life are concerned, farmers are right to protect their livestock by human means and try to remove those dangerous weeds themselves, as much as they can.

And, indeed, farmers have been fairly successful over the last century at doing just that—using weed killers to help them. There's no question that, where farming is concerned, weeds need a heavy hand. The sad side-effect, though, is that the diversity of all wild plants on farmland has fallen significantly as a result.

Seafaring weeds

Some of the world's best-known weeds have arrived far from their natural habitat—brought on ships from across the seas. Centuries of exploration, colony, and adventure have meant that knowingly or unknowingly, seafarers carried weeds on their ships, as well as vegetables, fruit, and meat-sources, introducing them to shores far from home. Weeds traveled from Europe to the Americas in the fifteenth century; and in the eighteenth century from Europe to Australasia. Once landed, and out of their natural habitat where pests and diseases may have evolved to keep them in check, rebel plants could find new and abundant life, reproducing in vast quantities and taking over to rule the roost. These, then, are rebels turned tyrants, rampaging through lands, taking over weaker species not in a trickle, but in an unstoppable flood.

This weedy spread has continued right up until the present day: it's only the turn of the new millennium that has seen humankind take significant steps to stem the flow of invasive species. Thousands of weeds, though, are now so widespread it is impossible to remove them, and some, such as Brassica species, can be a real problem for native plants in the US.

When ornamental plants rebel

Plant-hunting reached obsessive levels during the Victorian era, when wealthy land-owners funded expeditions to discover new plants and introduce them to ornamental gardens back home. However, these introductions were often made without anyone fully appreciating the growth habits of the plants in the new locations.

In 1850, Kew Gardens in the UK imported *Fallopia japonica* (see p.28), describing it as one of the most stately ornamental plants of the time. It was quickly distributed around the country via vegetative propagation—thankfully, the introduction was male, the plant being dioecious, needing a female partner to produce seed. This limited the rate of its spread.

Introduced to the UK as an ornamental in 1901, *Lysichiton americanus* became an illegal invasive alien species in Europe in 2016. This means that while you can still grow it under controlled conditions, if it's already in your garden, it's now illegal in Europe to introduce it.

Many plants we now consider weeds for their rebellious behavior began life in our soils in this way. *Linaria purpurea* (see p.60), *Oenothera biennis* (see p.72), *Pilosella aurantiaca* (see p.124), *Soleirolia soleirolii* (see p.110)—our recent ancestors brought all of these and more to our gardens, planting them because they thought they were beautiful.

World Wars I and II

During World War I, in the UK *Papaver rhoeas* (the common poppy) became the most recognizable and enduring symbol of those who lost their lives in this dark episode of modern history. Why? Because it was the plant that grew on the fields where troops had been killed.

The Blitz in 1940–41 saw German bombs level large areas of London. In among the rubble and devastation, though, came weeds—the first signs of new life from horror, symbols for a country that needed to begin its process of healing. Reports from the time suggest a widespread proliferation of *Chamerion angustifolium*, which seized its opportunity to colonize craters in places it had rarely been seen before.

Cities and the future

The factor that links all weeds—whether native or introduced; gentle rebel or marauding tyrant; medicinal or harmful—is us, humans. Weeds are a very human problem. A weed without humans is just a plant; whereas a plant that causes problems for humans is a weed. And this has always been so.

It will be interesting to document the course of weeds in years to come and what they mean to humanity in the future. By 2050 it's estimated that more than 66 percent of humans will live in cities, an unnatural habitat that we've created. Weeds appear to be the first plants moving into cities with us, adapting to this new environment. If our relationship with weeds has always been a close one, it seems it's about to get even closer.

Above: *Linaria purpurea* and *Leucanthemum vulgare*.

Ascension: When Rebels Become Good

There are some plants that by rights we should consider weeds, but somehow they've made it into our hearts and minds as garden plants—they've crossed over to the good side. Giving them labels like "wildflower" and "self-sower," somehow we gloss over the fact that these plants behave like any other weed. Here are some of these rebels turned good (Part Two makes a case for those weeds that we should consider alongside them).

Snapdragon • *Antirrhinum majus*
Commonly sold as a garden plant, *Antirrhinum* is as tough as any other weed, happily seeding into cracks in medians, walls, and any other dry, sunny spot.

Foxglove • *Digitalis purpurea*

Digitalis purpurea self-seed heavily in the right, usually sunny conditions. Without control, the plants will create vast stands of flowers. They are poisonous to humans if eaten. *Alcea rosea* behaves in a similar way in sunny spots, with equally tall spires of flower.

Mexican fleabane • *Erigeron karvinskianus*

This is another garden plant that exhibits rebel behavior worse than most weeds! Beautiful white flowers fade to pink throughout summer and fall, self-seeding everywhere. US native *Erigeron glaucus* behaves in a similar way.

English bluebells • *Hyacinthoides non-scripta*
Native to western Europe, in the UK, *Hyacintoides non-scripta* make beautiful, blue, woodland carpets. Away from the tough growing conditions of the dry shade of trees, however, *Hyacinthoides non-scripta* can turn problematic. Not to be confused with the native *Mertensia virginica*, also called Bluebells but an entirely unrelated plant.

Forget-me-not • *Myosotis sylvatica*
Myosotis sylvatica seeds itself around thickly, yet we let it off the weedy hook thanks to its beautiful blue flowers.

Primrose • *Primula vulgaris*
A clear sign of spring in the UK and some areas of the USA, *Primula vulgaris* will often pop up weed-like in lawns and damp, shady spots.

Great mullein • *Verbascum thapsus*
With soft, silvery leaves and tall spikes of yellow flowers during summer, *Verbascum thapsus* will make itself at home in dry, sunny soils.

Most Unwanted: Weeds to Avoid

While I believe all plants have their own beauty, some are hard to recommend at all, and some best avoided in certain situations. This is especially true when they are almost uncontrollable in their will to take over, which happens most often when we have introduced them to parts of the world where the native plants, pests, and diseases haven't evolved to keep them under control.

If you already have any of the following weeds, you could try incorporating them into your garden designs, rather than trying to fight them. Always do your best to keep them in check.

Maple Sycamore • *Acer pseudoplatanus*
Common along the East Coast, this is, without doubt, a beautiful tree. However, that beauty doesn't counter the sheer volume of the seedlings it produces every year, which it throws over such long distances. The seeds will float in the wind across an entire garden, and outside of it. This lack of control and how quickly the seeds grow into large, hard-to-remove seedlings mean I can't recommend it. Do not plant it and, while I hate to say it, remove established trees to replace them with other better-behaved trees if you are allowed to (often this is illegal, so do check).

Ground elder • *Aegopodium podagraria*

This is actually a very attractive plant with beautiful white umbels of flower like *Anthriscus sylvestris* (see p.104). It almost made it onto my recommended list, but it didn't because it really does spread thickly (especially in areas such as New England, the Midwest, and the Pacific Northwest), creating solid ground cover that, unlike smaller plants, will compete with many garden perennials. However, in tough spots where nothing else will grow and you're able to contain it, do consider keeping it. There is a variegated cultivar that is weaker and very popular among gardeners.

Hedge bindweed • *Calystegia sepium*

Large blankets of *Calystegia sepium* can actually have a classical beauty reminiscent of climbers in Renaissance and medieval paintings. Its pure white, trumpet flowers against healthy leaves look quite pretty. However, it's hard to train to grow where and how you like, and it spreads like wildfire through the ground. The smaller field bindweed is similar, but much easier to control with a hoe. Eradicate *Calystegia sepium* with weed killer brushed onto the leaves, or cover the area with weed-suppressant matting (see p.42) for at least two years.

Creeping thistle • *Cirsium arvense*
Thistles are beautiful flowers, but some, such as *Cirsium arvense*, are incredibly troublesome, particularly in meadows where they can run rampant. Dig out their deep roots, making sure you get all of them, and burn or dispose of the whole plants carefully.

Quackgrass • *Elymus repens*
Invasive all over the US except the Deep South, *Elymus repens* spreads via underground rhizomes and seed. Its young seedlings are relatively easy to pull out, but, once established, the rhizomes are very hard to deal with, spreading underground in all directions, sometimes deeply. The rhizomes will snap easily and careful digging can expose them so that you can get them out. But, any little piece remaining in the ground can regrow, so extract as much as you can see, then repeat the weeding process regularly so that you catch new sprouts as they occur.

Field horsetail • *Equisetum arvense*

Although I recommend the larger weed, *Equisetum hyemale* (see
p.122), in the book, this smaller sibling is a hard sell—despite its
lovely green color and bottlebrush shape. Where it's happy, which
is in most soils, it will spread rapidly and aggressively, appearing
everywhere. It's resistant to weed killers, which makes it difficult to
eradicate completely. Weed-suppressant matting (see p.42) will work,
but it will take at least two years to do the job and you need to be
sure you're covering every plant. Even one or two left in will quickly
re-populate an area.

Japanese knotweed · *Fallopia japonica*

Originating from eastern Asia, including China and Korea as well as Japan, attractive-looking *Fallopia japonica* was introduced to gardens around the world as an ornamental plant. It has been known to invade large swaths of land in New England, especially along river banks. Eradicate it using strong weed killer regularly injected into the stems. Also try covering it with weed-suppressant matting (see p.42) and keep checking for months after you think it has gone—it can regrow from tiny root pieces.

Fennel · *Foeniculum vulgare*

Gardeners in cooler, wetter climates may be surprised to see *Foeniculum vulgare* included in a list of weeds to avoid. It is, after all, a beautiful plant for its flowers, shape and leaves, making it outstanding for use in garden design—and it's good in cooking, too. However, in dry climates that are reminiscent of its Mediterranean home, such as in parts of Australia, New Zealand, and America, *Foeniculum vulgare* reproduces faster than many other native plants. However, on the west coast and some of the east coast use it with caution as it will spread rapidly by seed.

Himalayan balsam · *Impatiens glandulifera*
Found in New England and the Pacific Northwest, *Impatiens glandulifera* is a very pretty weed with beautiful, sweetly scented pink flowers. En masse it's lovely, but I'd recommend other tall, pink weeds before this one. It is incredibly invasive in areas, in damp soils and especially on the banks of streams, rivers and ponds, where the seed gets washed around. It blocks the sun to easily wipe out other waterside plants. If you want to grow it, keep the plant away from water where seed control is impossible; otherwise, it is actually very easy to control simply by pulling out before it sets seed. Repeat every season until it's gone for ever.

Japanese stiltgrass · *Microstegium vimineum*
Microstegium vimineum is an annual grass that has become seriously invasive in the eastern half of the US. It creates a dense blanket that outcompetes other plants. To remove it (which you should), prevent it from seeding to gradually reduce the population. Mow or hand pull the plants if the problem is relatively small scale.

Prickly pear • *Opuntia stricta*

Although a fantastic garden plant in the Deep South, the southeast, and central areas of the US, outside of its native habitat *Opuntia* spp. can be so successful in dry, warm, sunny environments that it spreads rapidly from seed. You can control this in gardens if you're diligent, but take your eye off it and it can form fairly large shrubs quite quickly.

Green alkanet • *Pentaglottis sempervirens*

More of a problem in countries outside of the US, *Pentaglottis sempervirens* has been spotted around Oregon and is the owner of a deep and stubborn taproot. Dig it out to eradicate the plant, making sure you get all of the root and keep repeating the digging and removing until the plant is gone. Weed-suppressant matting (see p.42) is also a good option.

Bracken • *Pteridium aquilinum*
One of Europe's largest native ferns, which is also native to the USA,
is beautiful, but it will spread quickly by runners, taking over all areas
of a garden. There is also evidence to show that its airborne spores
can be carcinogenic if you are around large quantities of the plant
for a long time. Regularly pull it out (it's easy to do so) until you've
eradicated it.

Kudzu vine • *Pueraria spp.*

A vigorous, weedy vine from East Asia, *Pueraria* was introduced to the US and other countries, as a means of stablilizing soil that was at risk of erosion. In places where it was happy it soon became highly invasive, especially in the Deep South. It grows so vigorously it can smother entire shrubs and trees, blocking sunlight and killing them. Weed killers will work, but it's better first to try regularly cutting off the top of the plant above the roots until it weakens and eventually dies. Strong weed-suppressant matting (see p.42) will work, too, but the large plant may find a way to grow around it.

Rhododendron • *Rhododendron ponticum*

One of the first ornamental rhododendrons to be planted widely by Victorians, with beautiful flowers and being strong growing, *Rhododendron ponticum* almost made it into my list of recommended weeds. With the right control, it can be fine to grow. In the US it's less of a problem but it does have a tendency to spread its seedlings far and wide. By the time you spot them, they may be too big. Remove plants entirely.

European blackberry • *Rubus fruticosus*

The wild blackberry has delicious fruit and is fine to grow if you
maintain it with regular pruning and you regularly rip out its runners
that pop up nearby. However, it's such a strong grower, it's very hard
to keep on top of it. In kitchen gardens you can try using root barriers
to control its spread. However, cultivars will produce more fruit, so
I question whether *Rubus fruticosus* is really good-looking or useful
enough to be worth the effort.

Part One

Bringing Weeds into Your Garden

Most weeds come to us, but if you've been patiently waiting for that one weed you lust after to no avail, it's time to act. Finding and bringing weeds into your garden is a fun, easy and rewarding activity. Contrary to popular belief, with a little bit of knowledge and some careful planning and control, designing with weeds can lift your garden from beautiful to glorious.

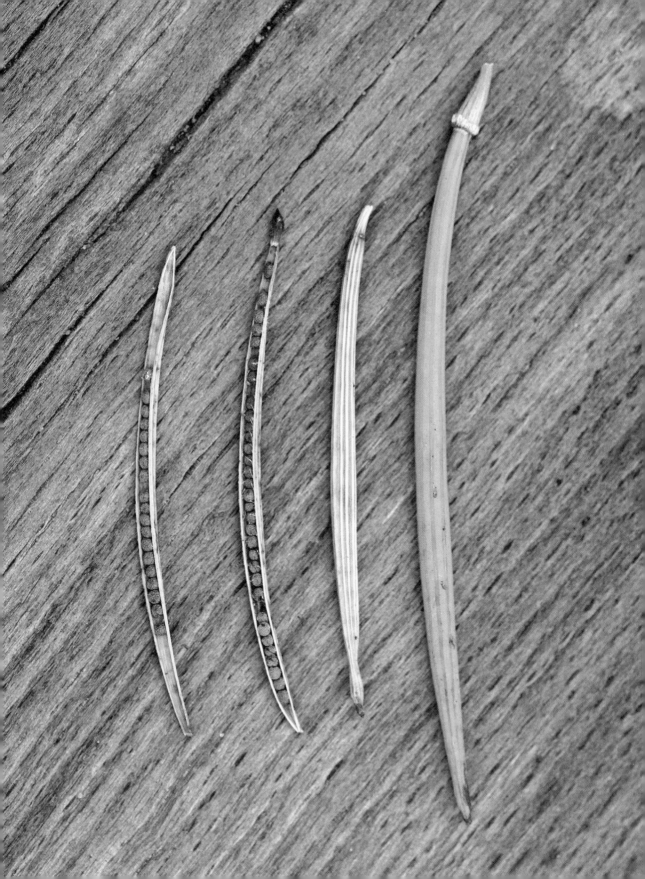

Weed Hunting

Previous page: *Digitalis purpurea, Lupinus, Lilium* and *Foeniculum vulgare*.
Opposite: *Eschscholzia californica* seed pods ranging from ripe and ready to harvest (left) to unripe (right).

One of my favorite pastimes is weed hunting in different areas. Weeds tell us so much about a particular place (its weather, climate, soil type …). Growing alongside other plants, weeds are an endless source of inspiration for attractive combinations of color and form. The sheer variety of weeds you'll see within a five-minute radius of your home or workplace is quite amazing. Discovering a weed in an unusual place is every bit as exciting as finding a rarer plant.

Weeds tend to grow in greater numbers near houses, because in the wild they are outcompeted by tougher plants. Keep an eye on front yards (these days a haven for weeds), along medians, in parking lots, on empty lots, and at the sides of railroads (obviously, don't go anywhere near the tracks themselves—weeds growing along them will be nearby in safer spots).

Next time you're at a friend's house, cast an eye over their gardens for any juicy weeds popping up. Even step outside and take a closer look. Each time I visit a new area, I make a point of peering into front gardens to check what's there. Residential areas are a particular goldmine for weeds, as there is such a high concentration of gardens and so many verges for them to jump between. Often, I find old gardens, let go over time, to be a Mecca for choice weeds, those that were once considered ornamental plants. Sometimes I wonder, were gardens invested as wildlife parks for rebellious weeds?

If you spot a weed growing in a sunny garden bed, keep looking as there will certainly be other sun-loving weeds nearby. Wherever I've seen *Oenothera biennis* (see p.72), I always also seem to find *Pilosella aurantiaca* (see p.124)—were they introduced to gardens at the same time?

Equally, shade-loving weeds will have set up home on the other side of the house. I've seen one sunny, south-facing wall with *Centranthus ruber* (see p.120) growing out of it, while on the shady, north-facing side, the wall was littered with different fern species (see p.148). And moss (see p.150)! Jackpot.

Almost certainly where you find *Digitalis purpurea* (see p.21) and *Viola odorata* (see p.136), you will also find *Lamium album* (see p.98).

Above: *Oxalis corniculata* var. *atropurpurea* seed pods.

If you're hunting for weeds for a drier spot in your garden, head for areas with sand- or gravel-based soils. Warmer areas with less rainfall—including towns and cities, which tend to have milder microclimates as a result of the shelter from buildings—and slopes and banks, which have extra light levels and fast drainage, are also good hunting grounds.

Weeds that thrive in damp soil will tend (unsurprisingly) to congregate near the coast or in low-lying boggy, rainy areas, such as valleys, ditches, and hollows.

Believe it or not, there is such a thing as a rare weed. One such plant is the vilified *Heracleum mantegazzianum* (see p.106)—you may need to do some research to find it. Look for news of local clumps that people have written about (usually in an effort to get rid of it). Where it does show up, its scale is unmissable.

With the exception of *Buddleja davidii* (see p.158), which widely makes cities its home, you will need to get out of urban areas to find shrubs. *Rosa canina* (see p.164) resides on hillsides and commons. Try searching empty lots to find *Lathyrus latifolius* (see p.160), although meadows or community gardens are often also a good bet. *Rhus typhina* (see p.162) is almost always in urban areas. Have fun hunting down this weedy shrub.

Collecting and Storing Seeds

Finding and collecting your own weed seeds is one of the best ways to introduce weeds into your garden. Embarking on the task, though, can feel daunting, especially as so often we buy seeds in packets with use-by dates. In fact, it's actually a simple and rewarding little task to collect your own seeds—there's no need for elaborate manufacture or packaging. And, importantly, collecting your own has the benefit of significantly reducing the chances of transporting pests and diseases from live plants. Some regions have regulations about seed collection from wild areas, so be sure to check beforehand.

Find your weed
First, though, you need to find your weed. Try doing this early in the year, while the plant is flowering so that you can identify exactly what it is. If it's in an obvious and easy place, say a corner you walk past every day, keep checking until the seed is ripe. If it's less obvious, or you might forget which plant it is if it dies back and turns brown, tie a little piece of pink yarn to it (okay, you can use any color).

Knowing when a seed is ripe
Seed is ripe only when it comes away fairly easily. This will be more or less obvious depending on the weed, but as a rule of thumb: a green weed is never ready. For example, *Papaver rhoeas* capsules will be fully brown and dried; Fabaceae (pea family) weeds all have pods with tiny seeds that are ready when they split open naturally; *Anthriscus sylvestris* (see p.104) seeds are ready when they are black and come away with a nudge.

Use small, brown paper bags to collect your seeds. Paper helps to keep seeds dry because it wicks away moisture, whereas plastic bags or foil will lock the moisture in. A paper bag also means you can write on it: label it with the name of the weed, the location and the date you collected it. Do your labeling there and then—any later and I promise at some point you'll forget what you have in your bag.

To sow or to store?
The time when a weed's seed is ripe is also the best time for the seed to fall to the ground. This might mean that the seeds start to grow immediately, or they might bide their time until the following spring. Aim to replicate this natural process: collect your seeds and then sprinkle straight away where you'd like them to grow. They may not

Above: *Lathyrus latifolius* seed pods.

germinate for a while, but they almost certainly will eventually. Alternatively, if your garden isn't ready, or you want to collect more plants before starting your design, you can store the seeds until you'd like to sow them. In particular, biennials, including *Anthriscus sylvestris* (see p.104), *Digitalis purpurea* (see p.21), and *Euphorbia lathyris* (see p.92), will benefit from having some seed stored. This is because the first sowing will form leaves that year; the flowers and new seeds will arrive in the second. For a constant display, therefore, you need to sow for the first two years in succession.

How to store your seeds
To store the seeds, fold the top of the paper bag over twice to keep seeds secure, then place the bag in a sealable metal tin, such as a cookie tin, which will limit the flow of air and is dark and cool. Seeds need oxygen to survive, but limiting it slightly extends the amount of time the seeds stay viable. Some seeds, like poppy seeds, will be viable longer than we're alive! I use a small filing box to store my seeds—I put the seeds into the hanging files and label them by sowing date.

Put the tin in a dark, cool cupboard. Don't worry too much, but the ideal temperature is just slightly higher than a fridge, so a garage, basement, or dry barn is perfect.

Moving and Dividing Weeds

Moving weeds

If you're impatient—and let's face it, with the prospect of adding new weeds, who isn't?—you can move fully grown weeds into your garden, rather than waiting for the plants to grow from seed. You'll get instant impact and you'll be absolutely sure of what you're getting. Some weeds (such as *Campanula portenschlagiana;* see p.142) have variable colors and leaf shapes. Check the entries on specific weeds in the book for advice, though, as some plants are better suited to moving than others.

Before moving a weed, check that it is free from pests and diseases. Look under the leaves for signs of distress—yellowing leaves, blotches, or white powdery mildew, or signs of bugs such as aphids. Of course, not all problems are visible, but at least those that are you can vet. Also, make sure to ask for permission before removing anything from private ground, and check local regulations—it can be an offense to remove wildflowers.

With that all clear, you can set about the move. Dig up the plant, damaging as few of the roots as possible. The roots provide the weed with nutrients, air and—most importantly when moving—water. Damage too many roots and plants are liable to struggle to draw up enough water to survive. Some weeds, such as ferns, have a mass of fibrous, thin roots; while others such as *Lathyrus latifolius* (see p.160) have a thick main taproot that can run quite deep below ground. Dig as far around the plant as possible with a spade or trowel to get a good block of root and soil. Keeping soil around the roots is important, because it protects them and contains tiny roots you can't see that are actually responsible for most of the absorption. If you take roots without soil attached, your weed will struggle. If it hasn't been raining, water the plant before digging out.

Place the plant carefully into a bag, pot or bucket to transport it, and plant it as soon as possible where you would like it. Dig a slightly wider hole than the plant looks like it needs, but make sure the plant can sit at the same depth it had at its original home. If you bury it too deeply, the plant can suffocate or rot; too high and the roots can dry out. Fill in the hole, firm the soil gently to make sure the plant is secure and the roots are making good contact, and give a good soak of water, as the plant will need it.

Dividing weeds

You need a substantial plant with multiple stems or growing points from the base in order to divide a weed. Water well and then dig up the plant. Carefully look where the roots and growing stems separate, perhaps scraping away a little soil, if required. Then, with a sharp garden knife or spade (I sometimes use an old serrated bread knife), cut the plant into two or more pieces so that each piece has a growing point and roots. Plant out the pieces where you want the plants to grow (that might mean returning a piece into the same hole).

You can also grow many weeds in pots before planting them, giving them time to bulk up before going into a busy garden bed.

Do bear in mind that not all weeds like to be moved or divided. *Papaver rhoeas*, for example, don't like root disturbance at all (so it's best to grow them from seed). See the individual weed entries for more information.

Above: *Campanula portenschlagiana.*

Managing Rebel Plants

Rebel plants have a tendency to be overeager to reproduce and need that enthusiasm checked from time to time. Equally, they are just as sensitive to life in the garden as ornamentals and require a little love from us to keep in shape.

Understand your designer weeds

One of the reasons I think humans resent weeds is that they come at us in great numbers. With such variety in garden invaders, it's hard to understand or see the best in any of them. I recommend, certainly initially, limiting weed use in garden design to one or two plants. This allows you the time to learn each weed's habits and growth patterns in depth, making each of your weeds much easier to control.

Growing rebel plants is really about understanding their life cycle, size, and means of spread. Once you understand a weed, it's easy to spot when it spreads, sets seed, or needs tidying. You can then add weeds to a design and maintain it with some basic controls without feeling any resentment toward the weeds at all. In fact, their very rebelliousness can become an advantage. For example, weeds can make the perfect low ground cover around larger, ornamental plants.

Keeping rebels in check

All that said, you will need to weed your weeds—that comes with the territory! However, it's easy to reframe this activity when you're not just pulling out unwanted devils, but reducing the numbers of plants you actually chose to plant (or keep) in your garden. Weeding is really no different to thinning out fast-producing ornamentals, such as *Allium sphaerocephalon*, *Monarda*, or *Nigella damascena*.

Weeds appear in conditions they like and then start spreading. Therefore, weeds require the opposite strategy to many garden ornamentals. Rather than pampering, feeding, and watering, weeds simply need restricting. Over the year this will take you significantly no more or less time than looking after ornamentals. Lightly cutting back a strong-growing, weedy rose every year or two beats spraying garden roses weekly for pests and disease. The care balances itself out.

Most weeds are easier to control than you may realize. The easiest methods of weeding are hoeing, hand pulling, and using a hand fork to loosen roots (or a garden fork for larger weeds). You must remove

Above: *Urtica dioica*, *Ranunculus acris*, *Anthriscus sylvestris*, *Fragaria vesca*, *Cirsium vulgare*, and *Digitalis*.
Opposite: *Aquilegia vulgaris*.

all of the roots, particularly on deep-rooted plants, such as *Taraxacum officinale* otherwise the plants will regrow. Other techniques to slow weed growth include deadheading before the plants produce seeds, and cutting the entire plant back to ground level to reduce its vigor. *Lamium album* (see p.98) is a good example, if it's proving too strong.

The only weeds I have found that can't be controlled with these techniques are those that, as a garden designer, I wouldn't recommend. Weeds such as *Urtica dioica* and *Calystegia sepium* (see p.25)—you'll find more on unwanted rebels on pages 24–33.

Removing excess or unwanted weeds

If we're choosing one or two desirable weeds for our gardens, we still need to keep their numbers in check. It goes without saying that lots of other weeds will hope to ruin our plans. Of course, you could decide some of these are also design-worthy. If not, below are techniques to get rid of them.

Remove by hand: First, cut back and dig out. Cutting back and hoeing weeds weakens them, and if you're hoeing correctly, you slice the plant off at the root, in most cases killing it.

However, hoeing is effective really only on young plants and seedlings. For more established weeds, you will need to dig out the root. This takes time so make a day of it. I find the best tools for the job are a hand fork for smaller weeds and a garden fork for larger ones. Slide the fork in near the weed to loosen the soil. If it doesn't come away easily, get your hand in and grab the weed as low as possible, gripping some of the root. With a slow tug, almost all weeds will pull out. Try it with a few and you'll quickly learn how the different weeds pull out of the soil.

Some weeds, such as *Calystegia sepium* (see p.25) and *Elymus repens* (see p.26), form rhizomes—roots that run underground in a network. Unfortunately, the only way to eradicate these is to dig and keep extracting as much of the rhizome system as possible. Every bit of rhizome left in the ground will regrow, but your repeated efforts will weaken the plants and after a few rounds of weeding, you will make a dent in their proliferation.

<u>Machinery for large areas</u>: On large-scale areas you may need to use a weed whacker or more powerful mowers to cut through plants such as *Rubus fruticosus* (see p.33), and rototillers to chop through roots. Cutting back weakens plants significantly and over time will kill off many of them. Be warned, however, that some weeds, such as *Elymus repens*, *Urtica dioica*, and *Calystegia sepium* will grow from fragments of root, so rototilling actually propagates many more!

<u>Weed killers</u>: Use weed killer only as a last resort. However, sometimes it may be necessary, particularly over large-scale areas of weed, or where the weeds are virulent and have taken over—for example, an area overrun by *Fallopia japonica* (see p.28), *Aegopodium podagraria* (see p.25), or *Calystegia sepium*. Remember that weed killers are poisons, so always take precautions when using them in bulk amounts. Some weeds may need more than one treatment, over time.

<u>Weed-suppressant matting</u>: A chemical-free, but longer-term option is to cover the soil completely with weed-suppressant matting that blocks all sunlight, eventually killing the weed. This is totally effective, but takes time—more than two years for some perennials such as *Calystegia sepium*. Although, if you concentrate on other areas of your garden while the matting is taking effect, it's amazing how quickly

Above: *Taraxacum officinale*.

time passes. Covering large areas of ground in matting doesn't look brilliant either. However, it's minimum effort, cheaper than chemicals and is guaranteed—all plants need sunlight to live.

Advanced weed-control techniques
To use rebel plants in garden design, it's critical that you know how to control them—that way, you stay in charge. One important technique is to block off areas where you want your chosen weeds to grow, and preventing them from spreading into areas where you don't. This is easier to do than it sounds.

Covering bare soil, blocking the life-giving light is one of the best ways to stop weeds spreading where they shouldn't. Options to do this include weed-suppressant matting (see above), but also paving, decking, mulches, and, perhaps most interestingly, ground-cover plants and dense garden beds.

Paving and decking: Good cement pointing or thin gaps between slabs, bricks and pavers will stop weeds seeding in between paving. A totally cemented area, such as popular polished cement, is impenetrable. Of course, this also makes the surface impermeable, so run-off measures are vital. And check your local guidelines: many areas have stormwater run off requirements and permitting for new hardscape.

Mulch: A thick layer (at least 2in/5cm deep) of mulch, bark chips, or compost will stop many weed seeds from germinating for a season. This sounds too good to be true, but works wonders. Perennials with established roots, on the other hand, will grow through with ease. It's a good solution after you've weeded an area to mulch, because soil always has a huge bank of weed seeds that mulch will stop germinating.

Barriers: Buried in soil, barriers stop the roots of weeds that spread vegetatively, such as *Lamium album* (which is related to mint and behaves in the same way; see p.98). The foundations of a wall, a pot (on a patio above ground, or sunk into the ground) are both good forms of barrier. For larger plants, such as *Rhus typhina* (see p.162) consider a 1–2 feet-deep (30–60cm) strip of Butyl rubber liner, which is usually used for ponds, buried vertically a short distance around the plant. Bury the liner as a barrier only around the roots, so that water can still drain under it. This is the technique many gardeners use for controlling aggressively (some might say weedy) spreading bamboos.

Ground-covering plants: Beyond thinning out and making barriers by hardscaping, my favorite technique for keeping weeds in check is to use other plants—removing any bare patches of soil so that there's no space or light for unwanted weeds to grow. Dense planting, with shrubs, closely planted perennials, and ground-covering plants that spread, all keep weeds at bay. We'll cover the detail of why this works and how to do it, and why the common practice of leaving bare patches of soil between plants is a terrible idea, in the next chapter.

Propagating weeds

Not all weeds last forever, many are annual or biennial. It's important to know how long your weeds will live when you're planning what to include in a design, so that you know how your garden will develop

and change. If you will need more of your designer weed for whatever reason—even weeds can sometimes struggle to be rebellious in a highly competitive garden bed—you can easily propagate them by dividing, taking cuttings, or sowing from seed. See pages 38–39.

Often, to be on the safe side, I grow back-up plants for my designs, at least until the gardens are established. Some plants, such as *Lamium album*, will produce runners, making it easy to cut off small pieces with roots. I grow them as "spares" in pots, ready to plant out as flowering plants if they are needed.

Above: *Leucanthemum vulgare*, *Trifolium pratense*, *Ranunculus acris* to the left of the path, facing *Pinus mugo* shrubs.

Nature's Design and Plant Communities

A new wave of gardeners is demanding gardens that offer more than pure beauty. The wealth of plant knowledge made available online and in books means that we have bigger ideas. Yes, we want color, but we also want something that's alive, free-flowering, and wildlife-friendly. And, in a time when well over half of the world's population lives in cities, the most unnatural places on Earth, we want natural. Many gardeners of today are plantspeople, intrigued by the way things grow and interact with one another in ecosystems. It's this knowledge of ecosystems, botany and plant communities that holds the secret of managing the beauty of weeds.

Plant communities

It's interesting that in the wild many garden weeds don't take over in quite the same way as they do in our gardens. They can't always compete with stronger plants around them: plant life is viciously competitive and in the wild, weeds fight for their lives every day. In gardens we remove this competition, creating conditions that are perfect for weeds: bare soil and breathing space.

Every plant receives energy, nutrition, and water from a combination of sunlight and the soil and air around them. In the ground nutrition and water are limited resources. Every plant sends out miles of roots to absorb and bring back essential, life-giving goodness. Sunlight is necessary for growth, and above-ground structures (predominantly the leaves) stretch and spread, like solar panels, to absorb as much as of it as possible. Look at plants in the wild and see how densely they grow with one another. Not a tiny square of soil is bare.

In the past in gardens we've tended to mollycoddle plants, going to great lengths to ensure they receive everything they need without taking from their neighbors and leaving gaps around them, which weeds squeeze into. Planting as a community means filling these gaps with plants you know will grow well together.

Many garden designers champion the approach of learning from how plants live and grow together in the wild. Piet Oudolf, Claudia West, Nigel Dunnett, and James Hitchmough are plantspeople who've successfully experimented with ornamental plant communities. Their dense plantings do require some maintenance (ensuring no single plant becomes too dominant), but the overall maintenance the plants need to thrive is far lower than in traditional, gappy garden planting.

I follow a similar approach in the gardens I design. I always think about the needs, size, and root-depth of the plants I want to use. I include various ground covers, which are essential for low-maintenance designs. These spread across soil, forming a mat that protects, locking in moisture and stopping other weeds from seeding into it. The most interesting ground covers to me are the ones with roots that won't interfere with other plants. They are the accommodating neighbors.

Understanding roots

Roots are interesting structures and as important to get to know and consider as the above-ground plant. They hold one of the keys we need to be able to create a successful, dense plant community. For example, *Hypochaeris radicata* (see p.82) has a very deep, and

Above: Ornamental *Rudbeckia fulgida*, *Echinacea purpurea*, and *Hylotelephium* sp. Opposite: *Anacamptis pyramidalis*.

Above: Silver and yellow *Verbascum* with *Taxus baccata* "Fastigiata" in a garden designed by Tom Stuart-Smith.

strong taproot that reaches deep into the ground, absorbing water and nutrients that other plants can't reach. This allows *Hypochaeris radicata* to grow among dense grasses and vigorous weeds, such as *Hirschfeldia incana* (see p.56) and *Centaurea nigra* (see p.80), which have a finer mass of roots higher in the soil.

In between, small ground covers, such as *Oxalis corniculata* var. *atropurpurea* (see p.134) have very short, fibrous roots that don't interfere with the larger plants—although they can form a dense mat to catch water. Ground-covering plants need light, even in shady spots, so growing among taller plants keeps them under control by also blocking their access to light.

Bringing plants together as a whole, considering how they can merge and interact with each other, creates a tight jigsaw in a garden bed. Strong plants will stop weeds from growing in the same spot, allowing rebels to sow around them.

Control using plant communities

To begin creating a designed community, think about your plants in layers, starting with the larger, stable plants. For example, vigorous, ornamental grasses, such as *Stipa gigantea*, *Calamagrostis* x *acutiflora* "Karl Foerster," and *Sorghastrum nutans*, form dense, impenetrable mounds. Also, shrubs such as *Ulex europaeus* (see p.166), *Rhus typhina* (see p.162), and *Cotinus coggygria*, once established, will have extensive root systems. Their stems will raise them above the perennials and annuals.

Around these add medium-size plants, starting with those that are well behaved; that is, plants that stay in roughly the same spot—try *Rudbeckia*, *Helenium*, *Salvia*, and *Eryngium*. Little by little aim to build up a patchwork of strong plants that will stand their ground without being too rebellious, not seeding or spreading too much. This patchwork of stable plants is the backbone of a community and begins to limit the available space for rebel plants to move around in.

Continue designing in this way until you feel comfortable with the amount of rebellious space you have left, into which you can introduce weeds.

Long-term management of a plant community

Plant communities are all about controlling plants by understanding how they want to grow and restricting their spread—it's the opposite of pampering and mollycoddling. Eventually, though, some plants may take over more than you'd like, while others start to dwindle. If this happens step in and remove excess numbers of the unwanted plant, freeing up space for more seeds or plants of the one that has dwindled. You may need to do this every year or two, but for the average-size garden, it won't take long. Eventually, in the long term, the time it takes you to maintain the garden will start to reduce, because the community itself will be blocking other weeds.

Ornamental plants in a weedy plant community

There are tens of thousands of plants suitable for growing in plant-community garden beds. To start you off some well-known plants gardeners use in communities include:

Echinacea
Echinops
Helenium
Perovskia
Rudbeckia
Sedum

Grasses include *Stipa gigantea*, *Molinia caerulea* cultivars, *Calamagrostis* x *acutiflora* "Karl Foerster," *Calamagrostis brachytricha*, *Miscanthus sinensis* cultivars, and *Deschampsia cespitosa*.

Growing conditions

Before choosing any plants, it's important to understand the conditions you're planting into. Here's a checklist to help you find out what you need to know:

Soil
Structure: is it clay, sand, loam, or a mixture?
Depth: how deep is the topsoil?
Fertility: how nutrient-rich is it?
pH: is it acidic, alkaline or neutral?

Sunlight
Exposure: think about the number of hours of direct sunlight a garden bed receives. If it's fewer than 6 hours a day, it's a shady garden bed.
Aspect: a nearby building or tree will affect the amount of sunlight a garden bed receives. A garden bed immediately next to a north-facing wall will receive no direct sunlight at all.

Water
Rainfall: how much do you receive per year compared with the rest of the world?
Retention: does your soil retain water or does it drain easily?

Temperature
Zone: depending on your gardening zone, how cold do your winters get and which plants can survive those temperatures? Equally, how hot does it get?

Care, effort, and rebelliousness

You will notice in Part Two of this book that each weed entry comes with a score out of five for three categories: "Care" indicates how much mollycoddling the weed needs in order to grow; "Effort" shows how much time and effort is needed to keep them in check; and "Rebelliousness" gives you an idea of how prolific they are at spreading about and seeding around.

Part Two

Weeds for Every Situation

Weed by rebellious weed, this section takes you through the rebels that I think deserve our respect and consideration. These are the weeds that perhaps—planted in the right conditions and given the right care and control—aren't that bad, after all. They might even lift your designs to make your garden, patio or balcony more beautiful than you intended when you first set out to populate it.

Chapter 1

Weeds for Colorful, Sunny Gardens

Everyone needs a flower garden bed filled with lively, long-lasting color from spring until the end of summer. Colorful garden beds usually have fertile, water-retentive soil situated in direct sunlight for most of the day, warm rays energizing the plants into pumping out flower after flower. This chapter focuses on weeds to grow in those full-sun garden beds alongside other plants, producing beautiful color for minimum effort—leaving you time to focus on the barbecue and cocktails.

Crow garlic

Allium vineale

The coolest gardens have plants with eye-catching shape as well as color: *Allium vineale* looks like nothing else on the planet, lending a cutting-edge, contemporary highlight to garden design.

Care: 0/5	
Effort: 3/5	
Rebelliousness: 4/5	
☠	

Plant family: Amaryllidaceae	
Max size: 47in (120cm) tall, 4in (10cm) wide	
Color: green and purple, occasionally with light pink flowers	
Flowers: May–July	
Pot friendly: yes	
Soil: well drained	
Situation: full sun	
Range: North America (USDA hardiness zones 5–9), Australasia, Europe, northern Africa, Middle East	
Origin: Europe, northern Africa, Middle East	

Gnarly is the word for *Allium vineale*. Its flower heads—about 2in (5cm) in diameter—of cool, contemporary, squiggly green set against a ball of dark purple on tall, thin stems are quirky attention-grabbers, reminiscent of balls of electricity.

In fact, what is on show here is not a flower at all, but a plant deciding to skip the flower stage to form an inflorescence of tiny bulbs, called bulbils. The green squiggles are the first leafy shoots of fifty or more baby plants starting to grow on the lollipop above the ground. Bulbs make up the purple sphere in the center and the effect, as the new shoots grow longer, is much like Play-Doh hair. Occasionally, the plant will manage to pop out the odd familiar *Allium* flower among the chaos, but that is rare and less impressive.

A real benefit of *Allium vineale*, like the popular, purple garden plant *Allium sphaerocephalon*, is that it's a late-season performer, showing off when most spring to early summer *Allium* have finished. Growing not unattractive grassy leaves from the start of winter, the plants sit tight until their display in mid-summer.

Allium vineale is a vibrant cut flower that gives a good—if slightly garlicky-smelling—filler for colorful flower displays. You can eat it, but apparently it has a less pleasant aftertaste than regular, edible garlic. Try it to see what you think.

Bringing *Allium vineale* into your garden

If you don't already have it, *Allium vineale* is easy to add. You just need to take some of those bulbils and plant them in the ground with the young shoots above soil level. Take from plants with the most impressive squiggles so yours do the same.

Allium vineale is best dotted through the front of a garden bed where you can appreciate the inflorescence up close. Like the garden plant *Verbena bonariensis*, *Allium vineale* will let sunlight through to plants sitting behind it thanks to its very narrow leaves. Try combining it with a backdrop of lighter color—such as those of *Nassella tenuissima* or *Festuca amethystina* grasses, or airy white-flowered *Gaura*, *Gypsophila* and *Cenolophium denudatum*—which will contrast the green and purple. Growing it against a white, cream, gray, and even black wall or fence would work really well, too—looking particularly good in urban, contemporary, and even tropical gardens. It would be interesting to grow it in a garden of lush, green foliage.

Invasiveness

In some areas of the US *Allium vineale* is considered a noxious weed and shouldn't be planted. If you have it and are allowed, grow with caution following the control tips. It likes to multiply—removing the weed from agricultural land can be very difficult. In gardens, however, it spreads only vegetatively, which limits its range.

Control

What you see above ground is also going on below ground with the parent bulb producing new bulblets beneath the soil. *Allium vineale* really, really likes multiplying. It's resistant to weed killer, which will run off the smooth leaves. It's because of this that *Allium vineale* has become a notorious weed in US agricultural circles.

In gardens, however, there's less need to fear. When the above-ground bulblets start to drop in late summer, cut the stem to the base and bin or burn them all (don't compost). Carefully dig and reduce bulbs below ground every few years. Consider growing the plants in buried pots or use buried Butyl rubber as a mini barrier (see p.43) to help contain below-ground spread.

Cultivated varieties

One cultivar is sold as *Allium* "Hair" but, really, there is no difference.

Queen Anne's Lace

Daucus carota

Daucus carota is one of the most structurally beautiful flowers in the world. Its gorgeous white flowers belie the fact this plant is none other than the weedy parent of the bright-orange root we eat for dinner.

Level of care: 1/5	
Effort: 1/5	
Rebelliousness: 2/5	
☠	

Plant family: Apiaceae
Max size: 35½in (90cm) tall, 12in (30cm) wide
Color: white, occasionally with a pink tinge
Flowers: June–November
Pot friendly: yes
Soil: well drained
Situation: full sun
Range: global (USDA hardiness zones 3–9)
Origin: Europe, southwest Asia, northern Africa

Daucus carota was cultivated into the edible carrot. If you dig one up, it will smell unmistakably carroty—although eating one of these is likely to give you a stomach ache. The entire lifecycle of *Daucus carota* is filled with beauty, starting with finely divided ferny foliage that forms a low mound. Large, flat umbels of white flowers, like plates of cloud, later emerge on tall, stiff stems (cultivated carrots have the same flowers). In the center is a single, central crimson flower. Beneath the umbel lies a designer collar of thin green bracts. As the flowers are pollinated and go to seed, the disks curve in on themselves to form spiny goblets (deadhead them at this point and more flowers will pop up). These, later, in fall and winter, curve in on themselves to cup the seeds. They look stunning covered in frost or a light cap of snow.

Daucus carota is a valuable cut flower that will last for at least a week in the vase and indefinitely if dried. Try adding dye to the water to change the color of the white flowers.

Did you know?
One of *Daucus carota*'s nicknames is Queen Anne's Lace. Legend has it that the single, central, crimson flower comes from the time Queen Anne (either the eighteenth-century English Queen Anne, or her sixteenth-century grandmother, Anne of Denmark) pricked her finger and a drop of blood landed on the otherwise lacey white blooms.

Bringing *Daucus carota* into your garden
Like many plants with a long taproot, *Daucus carota* doesn't transplant well and is best grown from seed. This is easy: the flower heads curl in on themselves when setting seed, eventually turning totally brown. The seeds are ready when they are held loosely within the flower head. At this point the dried seed heads look like tiny, skeletal hands holding seeds that are reminiscent of mini hedgehogs. Tip the seeds into a paper bag and sow a few where you'd like them to grow.

Daucus carota is an alternative to common garden bed plants such as *Achillea* and *Ammi majus* and their cultivars. The flower heads tend to be flatter than *Ammi*, although in a garden bed it's quite hard to tell the difference between the two. It's similar to the shade-loving, early summer weed *Anthriscus sylvestris* (see p.104), and, with its late-summer flowering period, can extend the effect for most of the year when the two are grown near each other.

Like all flat-umbled plants, *Daucus carota* works well alongside flowers of different shapes. For a dreamy display combine an airy plant, such as *Cosmos bipinnatus* or *Hirschfeldia incana* (see p.56), plus a plant with spires, like *Linaria purpurea* (see p.60), *Salvia nemorosa*, or *Veronicastrum*.

As a biennial, *Daucus carota* will produce the fluffy leaves in the first year and flower the next. Occasionally, it will flower again in the following year. This biennial nature makes it a good candidate for sowing in spring for two years running, to start a cycle of annual flowers.

The flat top of the umbel is the perfect landing pad for hoverflies and butterflies and its seeds may be eaten by birds in winter. However, it can also harbor carrot rootfly, a pest that burrows into the root of edible crops, so don't plant it near vegetable beds.

Invasiveness
Although easy to control in gardens, in some areas of the US it is a noxious weed.

Control
Dig out unwanted plants as you see them, digging deep to remove the taproot. The flower heads produce a lot of seed, so cut them off as they go to seed to prevent them spreading. Hoe or hand pull any seedlings.

Cultivated varieties
Daucus carota "Dara" has dark purple flowers that fade as they age, creating an interesting mist of shades. Occasionally, this variety will send up white flowers, too, adding to the effect.

Mediterranean mustard

Hirschfeldia incana

Thought to have been introduced to the Americas by the Spanish, as the common name suggests, *Hirschfeldia incana* was first cultivated for producing mustard oil— a use it still has today. The yellow firework-like flowers shoot off in every direction and mingle among other plants without blocking sunlight.

Care: 0/5

Effort: 2/5

Rebelliousness: 4/5

Plant family: Brassicaceae

Size: 39½in (100cm) tall and 39½in (100cm) wide

Color: yellow

Flowers: May–first frosts

Pot friendly: yes

Soil: well drained

Situation: full sun

Range: global (USDA hardiness zones 6–11)

Origin: Mediterranean basin (southern Europe, northern Africa)

Hirschfeldia incana may well be one of the world's most common weeds (especially in North America) but, like many brassicas (it is related to broccoli, cauliflower, and kale), it is architecturally appealing. It is a light and airy plant with dots of small, yellow flowers on long, wiry stems. *Brassica nigra* (black mustard) looks almost identical, as does *Rapistrum rugosum* (brilliantly nicknamed Bastard Cabbage).

Forming short rosettes of gray-green leaves at ground level, *Hirschfeldia incana* will send up many stems in all directions from May, then flower continuously all summer. The low leaf:flower ratio is highly valuable in a garden for maximum color. The seed pods tuck against the stems, giving the weed a neat appearance.

Bringing *Hirschfeldia incana* into your garden
In the US it is not advisable to introduce *Hirschfeldia incana* to your garden because it is so invasive when it escapes.

Outside of the US it can be grown among other plants in a hot garden bed, or in a tropical or romantic garden alongside other blendable plants. Greens and buff browns of ornamental grasses are perfect, as well as the orange, greens, and reds of *Kniphofia*, *Rudbeckia*, and large *Dahlia*. A beautiful combination is *Hirschfeldia incana* with *Leucanthemum maxima*—the yellow of the *Hirschfeldia incana* flower matching the yellow center of the daisy. For an exciting combination, aim for maximum contrast: *Linaria purpurea* (see p.60), spiked *Penstemon barbatus* "Twizzle" series, or species of *Echinacea*. *Salvia* "Nachtvlinder" has a floppy habit similar to *Hirschfeldia incana* and would blend really well with it as a result.

Invasiveness
Quite quickly one plant can become many! Problems arise when there's no control over the plant's spread or when soil containing its seed is cultivated, moving it around (the seeds themselves are heavy, so they don't run far). The seeds can remain viable for decades, which makes it hard to completely get rid of large populations.

Control
Although *Hirschfeldia incana* will readily seed around the garden, it is easy to control. Allow plants to grow only exactly where you want them. You'll see young seedlings forming around the site of the parent plant and control is a simple process of reducing them—hoeing or hand-pulling them occasionally.

Cultivated varieties
None known.

Tansy ragwort

Jacobaea vulgaris

One of the world's most outlawed plants, *Jacobaea vulgaris* is actually quite a unique and attractive plant. And, despite its ugly common name—tansy ragwort—it offers a magnificent weedy explosion of wildlife-friendly zing.

Care: 0/5

Effort: 3/5

Rebelliousness: 5/5

☠

Plant family: Asteraceae

Max size: 35½in (90cm) tall, 12in (30cm) wide

Color: warm yellow

Flowers: June—November

Pot friendly: yes

Soil: well drained

Situation: full sun

Range: North America (USDA hardiness zones 3–10), Europe, New Zealand

Origin: Europe

Jacobaea vulgaris grows bolt upright on stiff stems with only a little foliage, and tapers out into flat, wide clusters of tiny daisies in a rich yellow. Such horizontal structure in a garden bed is usually reserved for *Achillea* or *Sedum*. *Jacobaea vulgaris* is a biennial and will usually die after flowering, but not before scattering thousands of seeds.

In Europe, if you're lucky the plants will attract the cinnabar moth (*Tyria jacobaeae*), which relies on *Jacobaea vulgaris* to survive. The moth's stunning yellow and black caterpillars are straight out of the pages of *Alice in Wonderland*, yet the red and jet-black moth—as exotic and beautiful as any tropical butterfly—is the star attraction. *Jacobaea vulgaris* is rich in nectar and loved by other pollinators, too.

Bringing *Jacobaea vulgaris* into your garden
Jacobaea vulgaris seeds look much like dandelions attached to little fluffy wings, but held in much tighter clumps. Collect these when they come away easily and sow directly where you'd like them to grow.

Dotted throughout a garden bed alongside vertical spires of *Linaria purpurea* (see p.60), *Lupinus,* and *Salvia nemorosa*, or with clouds of pink *Astrantia* "Roma" and *Knautia macedonica, Jacobaea vulgaris* becomes a vibrantly colorful garden bed plant. It has an incredibly long flowering season from mid-summer until fall.

Invasiveness
In gardens *Jacobaea vulgaris* isn't that invasive, but is a noxious weed of wild areas. Do try to remove it if chomping animals are near you as it will irreparably damage the livers of livestock, particularly of horses.

Control
Jacobaea vulgaris's claim to fame is having its own UK parliamentary legislation, the Ragwort Control Act 2003, which exists to help limit the plant in areas near livestock. Gardens are another matter. It's not illegal to have tansy ragwort growing in your garden, but if you live within 300 feet (100m) of a field of horses or cattle do control its spread. (In the average garden, however, it's fair game—many garden plants are as poisonous, if not more so. In fact, the more poisonous a plant, the more interesting it usually is.)

Controlling it in garden beds is an easy case of ensuring other plants around it are strong and healthy, crowding out unwanted seedlings. And you should pluck out any seedlings you spot yourself. Toward the end of summer, rip out the old plants, or deadhead them, to control seed numbers (don't compost!). To eradicate, dig out the plants, or cover them with weed-suppressant matting (see p.42).

Cultivated varieties
None known.

Purple toadflax

Linaria purpurea

Linaria purpurea is an ornamental perennial turned weedy rogue. It is an easy, care-free plant, proclaiming purple towers of flower atop dainty silver.

Care: 0/5

Effort: 1/5

Rebelliousness: 3/5

Plant family: Plantaginaceae

Max size: 39½in (100cm) tall, 19½in (50cm) wide

Color: light to dark purple

Flowers: May–November

Pot friendly: yes

Soil: well drained

Situation: full sun, part shade

Range: North America (USDA hardiness zones 5–10), South America, Europe, Australasia

Origin: Italy

As far as weeds go, this one is easily forgiven for its narrow, silvery leaves that spiral up its long, elegant stems. Spires of purple flowers follow all summer. It is visually similar to non-weedy *Salvia caradonna* and *Verbena hastata*, but performs better.

Bringing *Linaria purpurea* into your garden

Linaria purpurea comes in varying shades of purple, so you need to select the color you want in your garden. Nab a plant growing in a median (not someone else's garden!) and replant it. Even easier, wait until late summer and tap some seeds out of the top of the plant into your hand or a paper envelope. Scatter the seeds around your garden and, sure enough, in time you'll see those telltale spiraling silver leaves.

Grow it as a clump of vertical flowers or allow it to pop up here and there for little accents of color among lower-growing plants. Over the years, as soon as you see the plants flower, remove those that pop up in your garden in shades you don't like. This will stop the plants cross pollinating. By this process of selection, you'll increase the color you do want.

Linaria purpurea looks stunning with pink or other purple flowers, as well as contrasting yellows, such as *Hirschfeldia incana* (see p.56). For a classy look combine it with airy white umbels of *Cenolophium denudatum*.

Invasiveness

If popping up across your garden in colorful purple towers is considered invasive, it's time to surrender. *Linaria purpurea*'s fatal flaw is its success. It reproduces so well that only a year after planting it, you'll find it growing out of gravel, paving cracks, walls, roofs, everywhere! Over time, many gardeners have backtracked on introducing *Linaria purpurea* to save on time weeding it out. What a waste!

Control

Easy: yank out the obvious seedlings when you see them. The plants shed seed for a long period in late summer making deadheading impractical as you'll cut off the reason for having them—unless, of course, you want to eradicate the plant from your garden altogether.

Cultivated varieties

"Canon J Went" has pink flowers; for white, "Springside White."

Penny Snell CBE

Vice President and London county organizer for the UK's National Garden Scheme, Penny Snell opens her romantic Surrey garden annually to raise money for charity.

Which are the worst weeds in your garden? Ground elder is a complete and utter nightmare; we had to leave and cover an entire garden bed. It's a terrible pernicious weed. We never used to have it until it arrived on box balls in their roots.

Are there any weeds that you quite like to grow? Teasels, where I want them I allow them and herb robert (see p.94) in gravel. Wild chervil (see p.104) seeds around the place. And another one I really love is creeping buttercups. They creep like mad, spreading like anything. I've lost the battle with buttercups. The other one is rosebay willow herb. I have the cultivated version, the white variety of it. I quite like the pink one, too, the one you see by the side of motorways, which will spread if you don't look out.

What is it about the buttercups that you like? Oh, I just love that we used to hold them under our chins when we were kids and say, "Do you like butter or not?" They used to reflect the sunlight—they're just the most lovely, joyous things!

Weeds bring back so many memories of sitting on the grass. Like making daisy chains ... Yes, that's right. My lawn was once one nightmare of daisies, which I quite liked, but then, when I first started opening the garden, I thought, I can't really have daisies on it. Although some people do, and they say they're meant to be there. But we crawled around on our hands and knees and dug them all out, so I haven't got any now.

When does a plant become a weed? If they're in a designated place it's fine, but if they pop up all over the place, then they're a weed. I let honesty seed around the garden. I've been known to go around the garden shaking the seed heads to grow more. A lot of people would call that a weed. In general, people call anything that self-seeds and is slightly uncontrollable a weed, when it's more about understanding the plant, really.

As an experienced gardener who's dealt with weeds more than most people, what's your take on weeds? Can they be controlled and do they have a place in the garden? It depends on the type of garden. People who are control freaks can't even bear a rose clambering into their *Wisteria*, they're up there and cutting it back. I think, oh gosh, let that rose grow. Those people can't have any kind of weed at all, nothing. You'll never find a blade of grass between their paving stones or anything like that.

What does a more relaxed approach bring to a garden? It's restful. People can wander around and needn't worry that they might be treading on something. It's charming when one plant twines through another; I don't think one should control nature too much.

Some weeds can be brutes, but do you think others are more useful, like herb robert? I've got that everywhere! One of our Hampshire garden owners gave me the white version, with little white flowers. It likes it so much here because my garden is incredibly dry and light and sandy. That little soft yellow Welsh poppy—people say that's a weed, but it grows in my garden in places where nothing else will grow, so it's quite nice having it. If you have a place where nothing will grow, perhaps a weed will.

When you open your garden, do people talk about weeds? People don't like evening primrose, *Oenothera biennis* (see p.72)—you see it all along motorways. I've got a very lovely pale primrose yellow one that is cultivated, but I think if you get the bright yellow one that grows everywhere that probably is a weed. The flowers do come out in the evening and then they're dead in the morning. They're quite hard work—I have to deadhead mine every single morning—but last the entire summer. I also have wild garlic. In fact, I dug it out from all the way down the side of my drive recently. It's a nightmare really, but half the people who come here don't see it as a weed, they just think it's a pretty flower. It's just in one place outside the gate now and luckily there's a lot of ivy there, too. Hopefully the ivy will win.

Of course, ivy is another weed. Yes! It's very invasive but it's another plant that does very well where nothing else will. It's a fun subject, you don't hear much about people cultivating weeds, do you?

Chapter 2

Weeds for Dry and Poor Soils

Life can be harsh for plants in areas that are dry and lack nutrients—areas that slope, or are made up of, say, sand, shingle, or thin soil over bedrock, or that suffer deep shade among drying tree roots. In these conditions only the toughest plants survive—step forward rebel weeds. Many of the most beautiful weeds grow in dry and poor soils—harsh environments can be stunning, too.

Teasel

Dipsacus fullonum

Dipsacus fullonum is a tall weed with large flowers that are useful for creating drama from summer through winter, as well as for providing food for birds.

Care: 1/5

Effort: 2/5

Rebelliousness: 2/5

☠

Plant family: Caprifoliaceae

Max size: 6½ feet (2m) tall, 19½in (50cm) wide

Color: green with purple

Flowers: July–September

Pot friendly: yes

Soil: poor dry soil; damp rich soil

Situation: full sun

Range: global (USDA hardiness zones 3–8)

Origin: Europe, northern Africa, western Asia

The flowerheads of *Dipsacus fullonum* look like they come straight out of a sci-fi film. Before flowering, the honeycomb of tiny buds is a fresh green with a metallic sheen, and enclosed in curved spikes. Then, in mid-summer, the tiny purple flowers open from the middle, forming two lines, one moving upward while at the same time the other moves downward. Bees absolutely love it, and in winter, in Europe, the seed heads form an important food source for the goldfinch.

Although the actual flowering lasts for only a short time, the architectural heads are around for ages beforehand, looking attractive in the bud stage. After flowering, they last for months, turning brown and standing strong all winter.

Bringing *Dipsacus fullonum* into your garden
Collect seeds in late fall, cutting off one seed head into a paper bag, which should be more than enough. Wait for the seeds to fall out into the bag or try shaking. Then, sprinkle the seeds where you'd like them to grow. Or, you can sow into pots to plant out later.

Although it enjoys heavy, damp soils, *Dipsacus fullonum* grows perfectly well in dry, nutrient-poor soil. These conditions help to contain its spread a little, too. *Dipsacus fullonum* fits well when you want to grow plants for their look when they die in winter. Plan for its buff-brown structure from fall. The plant holds its shape perfectly, the silhouettes of the seed heads standing out against other plants, especially tall, deciduous grasses.

One of the most beautiful combinations I've seen was in the garden of garden writer and plantsperson Diana Ross. There, *Dipsacus fullonum* grew in front of *Melianthus major* among tall, ornamental grasses, in this case *Calamagrostis brachytricha* and *Miscanthus sinensis*, hiding its base. This was early September with the onset of fall, and a few roses still had the odd pink and magenta flowers setting off the golden browns beautifully.

The plant is perfect for meadows and prairie plantings, too. Always try to grow something smaller in front of it to hide the basal leaves that look somewhat messy by flowering time.

Invasiveness
Dipsacus fullonum self-seeds profusely and in some states is considered a noxious weed.

Control
In the garden remove unwanted seedlings when you see them. You can cut off the seed heads in fall or early winter, which will limit seeds reaching the ground—but, of course, this also defeats one of the

main reasons to grow the plant! You could display the seed heads indoors where they will last indefinitely.

Cultivated varieties
None known.

California poppy

Eschscholzia californica

A contemporary-looking, invaluable little rebel, *Eschscholzia californica* brings easy pops of bright color for most of the year in difficult, dry soils in sunny spots.

Care: 1/5

Effort: 2/5

Rebelliousness: 3/5

Plant family: Papaveraceae

Max size: 12in (30cm) tall, 8in (20cm) wide

Color: mainly orange, sometimes yellow or white

Flowers: February–September

Pot friendly: yes

Soil: poor soil

Situation: full sun

Range: global (USDA hardiness zones 6–10)

Origin: USA (California and surrounding states), Mexico

Like so many weeds, the impossible-to-pronounce *Eschscholzia californica* suits almost every garden style: cottage, contemporary, urban, and even tropical. It rarely looks out of place thanks to its bright-orange flowers held over fine, glaucous-blue, soft foliage. Once introduced to a garden, it will pop up all over in those tricky dry spots with poor soil where nothing else seems to want to grow.

While you can try to sow its seeds in a specific area, like many poppies, *Eschscholzia californica* always has other ideas, often appearing on the other side of the garden. Best to let it get on with it, adding a sense of surprise and excitement to your efforts.

Did you know?
Eschscholzia californica has, perhaps unsurprisingly, been the official state plant of California since 1903. Herbalists use the dried leaves and stems to form a tincture or a tea to aid good sleep, although it doesn't taste very nice (the sign of a good medicine, perhaps).

Bringing *Eschscholzia californica* into your garden
Collect seeds from the long pods when they have turned brown and cracked open.

Eschscholzia californica looks stunning in mass plantings on stony, gravelly slopes, where its silky petals will flutter and sway in even the slightest breeze. Rock gardens suit the plant really well, re-creating its natural habitat on the stony mountainsides of California and Mexico. Planted in rock gardens, it looks at home against bare stone and will bring color among other small plants.

Grow the plant along the edges of gravel paths and driveways to add swathes of color. On modern properties its bright orange looks particularly contemporary, working well with grays and beiges. Plant it alongside the rich purples of *Salvia*, such as *Salvia nemorosa* "Caradonna" and *Salvia* "Nachtvlinder" for a particularly rich color combination. *Eschscholzia californica* looks good with almost every grass, too.

Invasiveness
Eschscholzia californica has the potential to be invasive in areas without much competition from other plants, but in a garden it's unlikely to take over, although it will pop up everywhere.

Control
Pull plants out by hand as soon as you see them. You can prevent the seeds from germinating if you cover the ground where they fall with a thick layer of mulch. Grow other, more vigorous plants over the area for the same reason.

Cultivated varieties
Various cultivars are available in different colors including white "Ivory Castle," pink "Rose Chiffon," and "Red Chief."

Common fumitory

Fumaria officinalis

An interesting-looking weed not often found in the US, *Fumaria officinalis* forms a small cloud of perfectly cut leaves.

Care: 1/5

Effort: 1/5

Rebelliousness: 2/5

Plant family: Papaveraceae

Max size: 8in (20cm) tall, 39½in (100cm) wide

Color: translucent pink

Flowers: April–October

Pot friendly: yes

Soil: poor soil

Situation: full sun

Range: global (USDA hardiness zones 3–10)

Origin: northern Africa, Europe, western Asia

Up close *Fumaria officinalis*, which is actually part of the poppy family, is an exotic thing with clusters of tiny pink flowers each with a dark tip that fades to almost white. When the sun shines through the pink petals of its flowers, the effect is one of the translucency of smoky glass. Get up close to appreciate it. Step away, though, and see the plant take on a different form. From a distance the tiny flowers and pale green leaves become less visible, merging into a mass that reminds me a little of the consistency of cotton candy. This wispy look is quite beautiful.

Did you know?

Fumaria officinalis takes its name from the Latin *officinalis*, meaning a plant for medical use. (A large number of plants use this specific epithet, including the common dandelion, *Taraxacum officinale*.) *Fumaria officinalis* has been given a whole range of medical uses, some with more substance than others—and it's worth noting that despite its success as a diuretic, for example, it's actually poisonous when ingested in large amounts.

Bringing *Fumaria officinalis* into your garden

If *Fumaria officinalis* grows near your home, you could put your feet up and wait for it to self-sow naturally into your garden, as it almost certainly will eventually. Or, find a plant in mid- to late summer that has seed capsules on it. Each capsule contains only one seed. Sow in spring where you'd like your plant to grow—*Fumaria officinalis* hates root disturbance and won't like being moved.

When you're deciding where to plant, aim to grow *Fumaria officinalis* between other plants with stronger shapes, such as vertical *Liatris spicata* and ornamental grasses or *Eryngiums*. *Fumaria officinalis* will act as a low, textured filler, highlighting the stronger outlines of the other plants. I've used it in tropical garden designs between large-leaved *Brunnera macrophylla* "Mr Morse" and *Fatsia japonica*. It worked particularly well with the *Fatsia*, as it popped out from behind some of the larger leaves, creating good contrast of color and shape between both plants.

On the edges of raised beds, *Fumaria officinalis* will trail down the sides by about 12in (30cm), extending the growing area. In general, it is best seen as a good front-of-garden-bed or gap-filling plant that accentuates those around it, while grabbing attention when people get closer. It would look particularly beautiful allowed to run rampant as ground cover throughout an entire garden bed filled with taller plants, including giant *Allium*, *Verbascum*, and *Iris*.

Fumaria officinalis grows best in thin, dry, nutrient-poor soils and will need full sun to look its most glorious. However, it will grow in many situations and suits coastal and cottage gardens well.

Invasiveness

Falling into the eager but not invasive category, *Fumaria officinalis* will self-seed very happily everywhere. However, it's small and doesn't compete with larger plants.

Control

You'll easily pull out *Fumaria officinalis* by hand, or else control it by covering areas with a thick mulch to stop the seeds germinating. Growing other plants to form a dense ground cover will remove the bare, open areas it needs to grow, which will also put a stop to it.

Cultivated varieties

None known.

Evening primrose

Oenothera biennis

Tall stems holding large, trumpet-shaped yellow flowers, *Oenothera biennis* rivals many garden plants for sheer, summer wow factor.

Care: 2/5
Effort: 3/5
Rebelliousness: 4/5

Plant family: Onagraceae
Max size: 71in (180cm) tall, 19½in (50cm) wide
Color: yellow
Flowers: June–September
Pot friendly: no
Soil: poor soil
Situation: full sun
Range: global (USDA hardiness zones 5–8)
Origin: North America, Canada

Oenothera biennis originates from North America and was introduced as a garden plant to many other regions of the world, including Europe. The common name, evening primrose, comes from the fact its flowers open fully in the evening, lasting a day before withering.

This is one weed that will happily grow anywhere in dry soils—in fact, it will make every attempt to do so. I first spotted it growing wild alongside railroads. From my commuter's distance, the large, bright trumpets of yellow were unmissable, looking positively tropical. It is a valuable plant for any garden and its flowers have a lovely fragrance from dusk.

As a biennial, it grows from seed in the first year, just like a foxglove. It forms a rosette of leaves that are followed by the tall flower spike in the second summer. Then, it sets seed and dies. The spike has a large number of flower buds along it, opening from the bottom up. So, although the individual flowers don't last longer than a day, they do keep coming.

Did you know?
Almost all of the *Oenothera biennis* plant is edible. The flowers make good additions to salads, and the seeds are used to produce evening primrose oil, which is found in many health supplements.

Bringing *Oenothera biennis* into your garden
Easiest brought in by seed. Sow *Oenothera biennis* where you would like it to grow. Collect it from the long seed pods from mid-summer onwards and sow directly either in fall or spring. It grows so easily from seed, the timing doesn't matter too much.

In gardens with dry, nutrient-poor soils, use *Oenothera biennis* in similar ways to *Lilium* or *Delphinium*, without the need for staking. Its bright yellow flowers combine well with the white flowers of *Leucanthemum maxima*, as well as other yellow flowers and contrasting pinks, such as *Dierama pulcherrimum* (which makes a particularly beautiful combination), *Echinacea purpurea*, and *Dahlia*. It also works well in a hot garden bed with the vibrant reds of *Crocosmia* "Lucifer," the orange of *Helenium* and *Kniphofia* "Ember Glow," and the yellows of *Rudbeckia*.

Rather than growing it in clumps, try growing *Oenothera biennis* dotted throughout a garden bed to draw the eye along, arranging the plant much as it would grow in the wild. Place shorter plants in between to allow the tall, yellow trumpets to rise above.

Invasiveness
Oenothera biennis is quite invasive in gardens because it produces a lot of seeds and rapidly. However, it grows only in poor, bare soils where it can get a foothold.

Control
Pull out plants as soon as you spot them to reduce numbers or eradicate completely. Don't let them flower at all if you don't want them because, like many invasive weeds, they produce seeds throughout flowering, rather than afterward. Planting in a corner where the plant is sheltered by dense hedges, shrubs or tall walls will help contain its spread.

Cultivated varieties
While cultivated varieties are hard to find, there are many species of evening primrose, a common one being *Oenothera glazioviana*. The flowers of this plant are almost twice the size of those of *Oenothera biennis* and the stems have distinctive, red-tinged hairs.

Castor oil plant

Ricinus communis

This is a showstopper of a plant. It is grown primarily for its huge, tropical, palmate leaves that come in shades of green to red (often a mixture of both).

Care: 2/5

Effort: 3/5

Rebelliousness: 4/5

☠

Plant family: Euphorbiaceae

Max size: 39 feet (12m) tall, 39 feet (12m) wide

Color: red seed pods

Flowers: July–October

Pot friendly: yes

Soil: poor dry soil

Situation: full sun

Range: global (USDA hardiness zones 9–11)

Origin: northern and eastern Africa

Growing rapidly and easily from seed, *Ricinus communis* puts on an astonishing amount of growth. In many cooler countries it is grown as an annual that can reach 6 feet (2m) tall in a single summer. The flowers are barely visible, but are closely followed by large clusters of round, spiky red seed pods that stay on the plant for most of the year.

Ricinus communis likes growing in drier soils, but can reach its supersized proportions only if given regular water and feeding. If you'd like to push it to its limits, try giving it a fortnightly feed of liquid seaweed and it may grow to more than head height with leaves well over 19½in (50cm) in diameter. Left to its own devices it will be happy, but the leaves will be smaller.

In warmer climates that don't get a frost, you can grow it into a branching, evergreen, large shrub or small tree. Once it reaches a certain size, the leaves will be smaller, but it will otherwise look the same.

Did you know?
Although the castor oil extracted from the seeds of *Ricinus communis* has been used for lubricating motor engines for more than 100 years, there's no escaping the fact that *Ricinus communis* is deadly poisonous to eat. Five seeds can kill a human: in the past assassins used the oil as a means to kill their victims. To grow it safely plant it far enough into a garden bed that people and pets can't reach it.

Bringing *Ricinus communis* into your garden
Ricinus communis develops spiky red seed pods that look like alien antennae. As the summer progresses, these will eventually start to dry, turning brown, splitting open and revealing three large, stripy seeds per pod. Split the pods as they start to open to collect the seeds. Always wear gloves and wash your hands afterward, because the plant is very poisonous when eaten (and it's better to be safe than sorry). To grow, plant the seeds in a pot inside in spring, 1¼in (3cm) below the surface of the potting soil. Soaking the seeds overnight before planting can help speed up germination.

Quite often you will see *Ricinus communis* as the central plants of formal bedding displays—alongside *Canna*, *Tithonia*, *Rudbeckia*, and *Solenostemon*. This tropical-style garden bed looks good and can be carried over into more naturalistic tropical or foliage gardens with *Ricinus communis* making an excellent feature.

Invasiveness
Ricinus communis will produce a good number of the large seeds each year, cracking open and landing a few meters from the plant. Germination rates are high, so the plant can quickly reproduce,

which in the wild can be a problem, as seen in California, where it has colonized vacant spaces, outcompeting native flora.

Control
In gardens its weedy ways aren't a problem, as it's easy to remove seedlings by hand (please wear gloves). Alternatively, place it in a sheltered corner, where the seed can't leap the garden boundary, or simply cut off seed-pod clusters.

Cultivated varieties
There are many *Ricinus communis* cultivars, including "Carmenchita," which has purple leaves and red seed pods; "New Zealand Purple" with very dark, shiny purple leaves and stems; and "Blue Giant" with enormous leaves and glaucous-blue leaves and stems.

James Basson — Garden designer at Scape Design

Multi-award-winning garden designer based in the South of France known for gardens inspired by natural landscapes.

What are your garden design philosophies and where do they come from? From landscape painting—not as a trained gardener; I don't have preconceived ideas about plants at all. When painting landscapes, what's the difference between sitting in a garden painting or sitting in a landscape painting? There's a logic to landscape: the tone of landscape changes as it nears water, for instance. This idea of weeds—it's not alien to me, of course, I'm a garden designer—but it's alien to a degree when it comes to appreciating a plant. Most of the plants I appreciate are in the wild and therefore all potential weeds in the gardens I design in the south of France.

How do you take a landscape and give it human context in a garden? In a way the only thing that makes our designed gardens look like gardens is the furniture and the lighting. What I appreciate are wild landscapes that allow you to sit in them. If you go into some brambly thicket, you don't feel welcome, but when you walk onto a caustic landscape, 50 percent of the ground is bare rock, the other 50 percent is this mass of dynamic vegetation. I'm really into these landscapes that are very poor in nutrients because that poverty produces space for humans.

Do your designs actually include weeds? Yes, potentially lots of the plants we use would be considered weeds, like *Cephalaria leucantha*. But these potential weeds are successful ground takers and super-useful in the garden, because they deal with lots of situations. We use *Brachypodium retusum*, a weedy but very good filling grass. It's not aggressive when it comes to volume—any other plant can elbow through it. It does a really good job of filling ground and dealing with shade and sun. I like to put plants across different aspects so you get variations in tone, even using the same species.

What are your favorite designer weeds? I really love *Hieracium pilosella*—this little ground cover is a stunner: furry, speckledy leaves with dandelion-like flowers. People hate it because it looks like a dandelion, but for us it's a winner as an unaggressive carpeting plant that gives another tonal texture to the ground. Once you stop thinking of these plants as weeds, they're like spots of paint you add to the planting. We use another grass called *Piptatherum miliaceum*, potentially super-aggressive, but this fountain of Champagne-sparkle flowers in the summer is another thing we love. And *Bituminaria bituminosa*: the leaves smell of bitumen, which is pretty gross, and gives it its name, but it's got character, flowering for us in late June to July. It's blue, flowering in a haze, a bit like *Verbena bonariensis* in a better way. Super-useful, but aggressive with a carrot root, you can't get rid of the damn thing if you don't want it, but if you've got the right level of water and soil, it becomes beautiful vegetation.

Are there plants in southern Europe that people should avoid because they are too invasive? No plant is off-limits if it's in the right setting. I don't think I have any plant that won't work. As soon as you're planting in 2in (5cm) of sand on concrete slabs, a plant becomes this delicate thing that can work. We had another native grass that we love, *Brachypodium phoenicoides*. In fields it grows to 15½–19½in (40–50cm) with a good prairie look, but in one garden it was so aggressive that we had to pull out the whole planting palette. It was running like a quackgrass, shouldering everything out because it had the right conditions to make it the biggest bully in the park.

How can people plan a garden when some plants don't stay in the same place? We start with a planting plan, using matrices of plants that drift across the landscape, and the percentage of plant changes relative to the conditions. We have structural plants that don't move, giving general structure to the planting, and then we have other plants that self-seed and merge to create areas of vegetation that are allowed to wander where the plants are happiest. Really gardens never stop changing. We want to work with gardeners who are into creative management—for example, who like selective weeding—and sculptural pruning, keeping character.

What is it about naturalistic garden designs that's so exciting? People have become romantic about wild space; it is zeitgeist romanticism about the landscape we're losing. People seem to have accepted the dead bits in gardens. Before, it was like "It's dead therefore it's untidy," and now it's seen as part of life. It's not for everyone, it's still quite avant-garde. Not everyone is going crazy because there's this brown prairie in front of their garden all summer—but it's coming.

Chapter 3

Weeds for Meadows

In recent years people have begun to better appreciate meadows as design features within gardens. Unlike traditional garden beds, meadows are dense plant communities where plants grow into each other, blurring edges into a living masterpiece, a sort of horticultural Monet painting. You'll find meadows on damp and rich soils, but most have low-nutrient, thin soils in full sunlight. Plants within them—such as the grasses that form the canvas—are tough, battling each other in an ever-changing war for space. Weeds excel in meadows, bringing layer upon layer of easy color as though an artist has smudged paints across their palette.

Common knapweed

Centaurea nigra

An indispensible, slender meadow weed that brings height with its colorful flowers, *Centaurea nigra* can be badly behaved but it's still one of the most stylish plants you could choose for your garden. It is an excellent source of nectar for pollinators; butterflies love it.

Care: 1/5

Effort: 2/5

Rebelliousness: 3/5

☠

Plant family: Asteraceae

Max size: 39½in (100cm) tall, 19½in (50cm) wide

Color: purple-pink, rarely white

Flowers: June–September

Pot friendly: no

Soil: any very well drained

Situation: full sun

Range: global (USDA hardiness zones 7–10)

Origin: Europe

It's worth introducing even a small, meadowy area purely to grow *Centaurea nigra*, with its splashes of pink and purple high above the grasses. This perennial forms quite rigid, upright stems that are narrow and somewhat transparent, reminiscent of the garden plant *Verbena bonariensis*, albeit shorter in height. The leaves are linear, sitting opposite one another up the stems. Tiny white hairs give the plant an attractive, silvery green color; and orbs of tight, dark buds with little black scales form a pleasing, geometric, pineapple pattern.

Interestingly, the flower can appear in two forms. The first form has little tufts of pink or purple above the bud, giving it the look of a non-spiky thistle and a fiber-optic cable. In its second form, the outermost petals (actually tiny flowers clustered together and called florets) extend outward creating the plant's most extravagant look, like small spaceships. Both forms are very useful: the thistle version looks sleek with dots of color accentuating the black bud behind; the wider-petalled form looks modern, sharp, and full of color.

Bringing *Centaurea nigra* into your garden
The best way to introduce *Centaurea nigra* is to sow the seed directly onto bare patches of soil, or into pots to plant out later. You can sow any time, although it's best to avoid the winter.

Collect seeds when the plants have turned brown and the slightly fluffy seeds come away easily. You can also buy seeds (and plants), but the flower is so common in meadows and the seeds are so easy to pinch off the tops, there's really no need.

Combining well with plants of almost any color, including yellows (try *Ranunculus acris*, see p.86) and whites, *Centaurea nigra* is an excellent and exciting backbone to any meadow. Grasses flow into *Centaurea nigra* and meadow climbers such as *Lathyrus latifolius* (see p.160) and *Vicia cracca* will scramble up it. In combination with *Leucanthemum maxima* and the white umbels of *Cenolophium denudatum* or *Achillea millefolium*, the dark purple will create a classy color palette. As a bonus, when dead, *Centaurea nigra* has a good winter structure.

Invasiveness
Given bare ground, the seeds of *Centaurea nigra* will successfully and quickly develop into plants and you can soon find them filling your meadow. In the USA, *Centaurea nigra* is considered an invasive weed (and is listed as noxious in Washington), and even across its native Europe it can successfully outcompete other plants.

Control
Pull out plants by hand before they produce seeds, being sure to remove the roots completely. This is slightly easier when the plant is larger and you can get a good grip.

Cultivated varieties
Centaurea nigra "Alba" has white flowers, but it is hard to get hold of.

Cat's ear

Hypochaeris radicata

Hypochaeris radicata is like the result of a garden designer taking a dandelion and reinventing it. It has all the beauty of those bright yellow flowers, but they sit atop a more refined plant.

Care: 1/5

Effort: 3/5

Rebelliousness: 4/5

☠

Plant family: Asteraceae

Max size: 12in (30cm) tall, 4in (10cm) wide

Color: pale yellow

Flowers: May–October (mainly toward the end of summer)

Pot friendly: yes

Soil: any well drained

Situation: full sun

Range: global (USDA hardiness zones 3–11)

Origin: Europe, Asia, northern Africa

One year I became obsessed with the common dandelion, *Taraxacum officinale*. Magnificent, bright yellow flowers and the delicate mathematical marvel of the seed-head clocks are second-to-none. Yet lower down sit chunky, straw-like stalks and tatty, lettuce-like leaves. No flower combines well with dandelions. I started thinking that there must be a plant with similar flowers but a designer body to match. *Hypochaeris radicata* is it.

It was introduced into western Canada at some point in the late-eighteeth century, spreading quickly throughout North America and, indeed, the world. A daintier cousin of the dandelion, *Hypochaeris radicata* and dandelion are often hard to tell apart. *Hypochaeris radicata* has similar, yet smaller flowers that are a shade paler. Its leaves grow in a typical dandelion rosette, but are smaller, thicker, and slightly hairy, making them tidier; and the flower stalk (the penduncle) is branched with more than one flower on each stem.

Stems are the width of a wire and long, blending easily into meadow grasses. *Hypochaeris radicata*'s greatest asset is that grass largely hides the tiny leaf rosette, while the wiry stem holds the flowers aloft, as if floating over or alongside the other meadow plants.

Bringing *Hypochaeris radicata* into your garden

Dig up a plant's complete taproot and replant it; or wait for the seeds, collect them and scatter them around. *Hypochaeris radicata* likes dryish, nutrient-poor soils and full sun, which means it is best suited to a meadow where the grasses aren't so vigorous as to grow tall and shade out the plant. To help keep the vigor of meadow grass under control, it is also worth introducing *Rhinanthus minor*. It is a hemiparasitic plant, which attaches to grass roots, leaching nutrients and stunting the growth of grass.

In a meadow *Hypochaeris radicata* looks good with complementary colors: buff grass flowers and green leaves help soften the yellow and create a relaxed, classy look that's somewhat romantic. Grasses work as companions because the airy and often vertical or arching flowerheads contrast well with the solid yellow, disk-shaped flowers. One of Europe's native grasses, *Briza media* looks particularly good with *Hypochaeris radicata*.

Other yellows will work, too, from *Ranunculus acris* (see p.86) to the white and yellow of *Bellis perennis* (see p.118). Orange is a complementary color to yellow, but there aren't many orange meadow flowers, except perhaps *Eschscholzia californica* (see p.68), which works in particularly poor and shallow soils with short grass. Closely related *Pilosella aurantiaca* (see p.124) should technically work, but the two plants are so similar in form that visually they can compete too much. To make a meadow more exciting, pair yellow with contrasting

purples, violets and pinks—a combination that happens naturally in the wild all the time. Try *Hypochaeris radicata* alongside *Lathyrus latifolius* (see p.160), *Vicia cracca*, *Lathyrus nissolia*, and *Trifolium pratense* (see p.88). Or, even try *Gladiolus communis* subsp. *byzantinus*. If you're lucky to have them, wild orchids, such as *Anacamptis pyramidalis*, which is found across Europe, will look perfect with *Hypochaeris radicata*. For a real clash it would be interesting to grow *Hypochaeris radicata* alongside the pale blue cornflower, *Centaurea cyanus*.

Invasiveness

Hypochaeris radicata is not hugely invasive, but it will spread where it can by runners and seeds. Once in your meadow, it will pop up here and there from time to time. Like the dandelion it has a deep taproot, making it hard to dig out completely. It is considered a noxious weed in Washington.

Control

Use a hand trowel to loosen the soil around the taproot as deeply as you can. Then, clasp the root as firmly as possible to lift out slowly. If you leave any root behind, the plant will almost certainly grow back. If you have the plant on a small scale, you can cut off the spent flower stalks at the base before the plant seeds around.

Cultivated varieties

There aren't cultivated varieties, but there are many different species of plant that all look similar. Try to see if you can spot the differences, as you may find a form of plant you would prefer in your garden. For example, *Hieracium pilosella* is a particularly attractive plant with rounded, small leaves; while *Leontodon autumnalis* is very similar and flowers a little later, extending the season.

Ox-eye daisy

Leucanthemum vulgare

If *Anthriscus sylvestris* tells us that spring has arrived, *Leucanthemum vulgare* announces summer. A supersized alternative to the common English daisy, *Leucanthemum vulgare* is a bright and fun showstopper, especially when grown en masse.

Care: 1/5

Effort: 3/5

Rebelliousness: 3/5

☠

Plant family: Asteraceae

Max size: 29½in (75cm) tall, 19½in (50cm) wide

Color: white

Flowers: May–September

Pot friendly: yes

Soil: any

Situation: full sun, part shade

Range: global (USDA hardiness zones 3–8)

Origin: Europe, Russia

There's nothing happier than a sweep of giant, bright daisies bobbing in the breeze along roadsides and pathways. Pure, bright, white petals and a solid yellow central disk make for a beautiful and cheery plant. Most commonly known as the ox-eye daisy, it is also called the moon daisy, because (like many white flowers) *Leucanthemum vulgare* will glow in moonlight.

As with many of the best meadow weeds, *Leucanthemum vulgare*'s flowers are held atop long, thin stems that merge well with other similarly structured plants, such as *Centaurea nigra* (see p.80). Its daisies are among the largest flower heads in meadows, which means they contrast nicely with differently shaped flowers, particularly from plants where the flowers form like masses of clouds.

When you see spent flowers, cut them off near the base and the plant will fire up more (although this strategy isn't particularly practical in a large-scale meadow, of course).

Did you know?
You can eat the flowers raw—they make a bright addition to salads or desserts. Try pickling the unopened buds and eating them as you would capers.

Bringing *Leucanthemum vulgare* into your garden
Collect seeds from the plant in late summer or fall, or dig up a young plant in spring before it has fully grown and flowered. Technically, of course, you could dig up any size plant as long as you're left with enough undamaged root ball for replanting. You can also buy *Leucanthemum vulgare* as plugs in garden centers or online.

Plant, or sow the seeds straight away in a sunny, well-drained patch of low-nutrient soil. In a meadow scrape away a bare patch of soil about 12in (30cm) square and keep it free from other weeds until *Leucanthemum vulgare* is established. Alternatively, you can sprinkle the seeds around in small patches of soil.

Leucanthemum vulgare looks best grown with a lower layer of vibrant yellows running through it from, say, *Ranunculus acris* (see p.86) and *Hypochaeris radicata* (see p.82). These flowers will bring out the yellow of the daisy's central disk. It also works well with the subtle array of flowers provided by the sprawling *Hirschfeldia incana* (see p.56).

As a short-lived perennial, after a number of years, *Leucanthemum vulgare* will eventually die to be replaced by its offspring. Spreading by seed is its best method of reproduction, quickly increasing numbers of plants and the size of the area it colonizes.

Invasiveness
Listed as a noxious week in some states, *Leucanthemum vulgare*'s main method of invasion is via seed: a single, established plant can produce many thousands of seeds each year. It will also spread slowly above ground via runners, which root and start new plants.

Control
Remove the plants before they set seed. Their roots are quite shallow and fibrous, but do make sure you get them all. Seeds already in the soil will remain viable for a number of years, so you will need to keep up removal annually until you're sure the plant is wiped out.

Cultivated varieties
"May Queen" is hard to get hold of and is reportedly sterile, preventing the plant reproducing from seed.

Meadow buttercup

Ranunculus acris

Ranunculus acris is a perfect example of a beautiful plant that has developed a bad reputation just because, at some point, it was classified as a weed. It is a perennial plant that stays green through winter.

Care: 1/5

Effort: 3/5

Rebelliousness: 3/5

☠

Plant family: Ranunculaceae

Max size: 39½in (100cm) tall, 19½in (50cm) wide

Color: Yellow

Flowers: April–October

Pot friendly: yes

Soil: any slightly damp

Situation: full sun to part shade

Range: global (USDA hardiness zones 4–8)

Origin: Europe, Asia

In the UK, we've all grown up familiar with meadows of *Ranunculus acris*. As joyful a scene as it is, it's easy to take for granted the lush green of grass dotted with bright yellow. I was reminded of this outside Chartwell House in southern England, once the home of Winston Churchill. Here, in spring, waves of buttercups turned the valley a glowing yellow–green. Nothing else looked so fresh.

To understand the plant's strengths, let's start with *Ranunculus acris*'s growth habit. Unlike other common buttercups, it has the much-sought-after quality of growing tall and slender, covering a large space without blocking light to other plants. Strong, wiry, near-leafless stems grow up to 3 feet (1m) tall, branching and ending with the glossy, bright yellow buttercup flowers. Like those of so many weeds, the flowers appear with warm weather: *Ranunculus acris* flowers from April through to late October. Its sparse leaves each have three finely cut lobes. All in all, it's a lightweight, airy plant that packs a punch of lively color.

Ranunculus acris prefers slightly moist soils that never quite dry out. If you have particularly dry soil, try *Ranunculus bulbosus*, which is more likely to succeed as it stores moisture and nutrients in its bulb-like swollen stem. It's not as graceful as *Ranunculus acris*, but the flowers are very similar.

Bringing *Ranunculus acris* into your garden
As flowers finish they develop into obvious seed heads with clusters of seed pods in a little globe. They aren't ready to collect while they're still green, so keep an eye on them and once they turn brown, try gently brushing the seed pods into your hand. If they come away easily, they're ripe. Collect them in a paper bag, then scatter them around your meadow and wait for the magic to happen. If you're impatient, dig up a plant and replant it.

If you intend to plant in an established meadow, it may be better to raise your plants from seed in pots, or to transfer older plants, to help them compete. However, in reality *Ranunculus acris* is unlikely to struggle.

Grown through a meadow, *Ranunculus acris* creates a sheen of bright yellow. With the bright white of *Leucanthemum maxima* it creates a joyful summer scene. For more excitement in your color combinations, pair *Ranunculus acris* with contrasting *Trifolium pratense* (see p.88), *Centaurea nigra* (see p.80), or other purples and pinks.

In spring, you could achieve interesting and contrasting shape combinations with large-flowered, yellow daffodils; or contrast color and shape with purple *Fritillaria meleagris* or *Crocus tommasinianus* cultivars, such as "Ruby Giant." *Gladiolus communis* subsp. *byzantinus*, with its rich magenta flower spikes, also contrasts well. Try

dotting some larger shrubs within the meadow: a tree peony with rich magenta flowers would contrast magnificently in flower shape, size and color; *Ulex europaeus* (see p.166) would complement.

Invasiveness
Considered a noxious weed in Montana, *Ranunculus acris* spreads via seed and it is only really a problem when it appears in land used for agriculture. The plant is poisonous to livestock (causing inflammation of the throat and gut), although instinctively animals will usually avoid it where other food is available. But, of course, this means they eat everything else around it, which clears the land and helps the plant's spread.

Control
Like most meadow plants, once established *Ranunculus acris* will be hard to eradicate completely, although removing plants and their roots will help reduce numbers.

Cultivated varieties
"Flore Pleno" has double flowers that look blowsier, but are less pollinator-friendly, because nectaries have been bred into secondary petals.

Red clover

Trifolium pratense

Trifolium pratense forms small clumps of green leaves and, throughout most of the year, provides pink–purple tufts of flowers. But, the main reason to grow it is for the fluffy bumble bees that love it so much.

Care: 1/5

Effort: 3/5

Rebelliousness: 3/5

Plant family: Fabaceae

Max size: 23½in (60cm) tall, 23½in (60cm) wide

Color: Pink

Flowers: May–November

Pot friendly: yes

Soil: any

Situation: full sun to part shade

Range: global (USDA hardiness zones 3–8)

Origin: Europe, Africa, western Asia

Trifolium pratense is a pretty little weed, perfect for low-growing color set against other meadow plants. The flowers provide problem-free color and they are short, which is perfect for pollinators. Seeing bees bumbling from one tufted flower head to another is a happy sight and brings a relaxing buzz of sound into a meadow.

The botanical name, *Trifolium pratense*, comes from its trifoliate leaves—*tri* meaning three and *foliate* meaning leaves (a four-leafed clover is a quadrifoliate). *Trifolium pratense* is related to common garden peas and other beans. Look closely at the seed head and you'll find miniature pea-like pods that contain a single seed. Like other members of this family, *Trifolium pratense* has the ability to absorb nitrogen from the air and then store it in nodules along the roots. You can see these nodules if you dig up a plant carefully and look very closely, ideally with a magnifying glass.

Did you know?
The notion of the lucky four-leafed clover originates from Ireland. The fourth (lucky) leaf arises as a result of a mutation—and, in fact, that mutation can cause more leaves than just four. Such mutations are fairly common occurrences in the plant world, but don't let that ruin the magic. If you manage to spot a four-leafed clover, you will have been lucky indeed.

Bringing *Trifolium pratense* into your garden
Collect the seeds in late summer and in fall, when the flowers have become seed heads. You'll know they're ready once they're brown. Rub them lightly between your fingers and they should crumble easily into your hands. Sprinkle the seeds onto patches of bare soil.

In design terms, *Trifolium pratense* injects life into a meadow by encouraging wildlife; its pink flowers giving the meadow an overall warmer glow. From a distance the flowers hold their color and offer a solid shape against finer grasses; up close the intense pink helps us to appreciate their detailed structure.

Invasiveness
Although highly invasive all around the world, *Trifolium pratense* isn't considered to be as rogue as larger plants, those that are poisonous to livestock, or those that ruin crops. It's invasive because, once established, it will spread readily throughout meadows. In its non-native regions of North America, Australia, and New Zealand, *Trifolium pratense* outcompetes other, smaller plants.

Control
Without using weed killer, it is very difficult—if not impossible—to control *Trifolium pratense* once it's established. That said, it's already so prolific around the world, it's unlikely anyone would now consider

trying to eradicate it. As with other small, sun-loving plants, growing larger plants that will outcompete it will help to slow down its spread.

Cultivated varieties
For white flowers, you can try *Trifolium repens*.

Chapter 4

Weeds for Shady Gardens

There are so many plants that have evolved to enjoy life out of the sun, and weeds that naturally grow in shade are among them. These exciting plants present us with the option to create a lush and colorful shady garden bed, bringing to life spaces in the garden that may otherwise go unnoticed.

Caper spurge

Euphorbia lathyris

Euphorbia lathyris is one of the most structural plants available to a gardener. Owing to its biennial growth habit, it is also possible to predict its size. This means you can make the most of its low, perfect foliage one year, then its tall, standout flowers the next.

Care: 1/5

Effort: 2/5

Rebelliousness: 2/5

Plant family: Euphorbiaceae

Max size: 47in (120cm) tall, 19½in (50cm) wide

Color: acid green

Flowers: March–May

Pot friendly: yes

Soil: any

Situation: full sun to part shade

Range: global (USDA hardiness zones 5–10)

Origin: central Asia to Pakistan, China to northern Vietnam

Euphorbia is one of the world's largest plant genuses with around 2,000 species. You'll see them as tiny weeds all over the place, but also as everything from cultivated flowers through to succulent, cacti-like plants growing in African and central American deserts.

Euphorbia lathyris looks like a plant from the future. When it emerges in its first year, it forms a short, vertical spike between about 12in (30cm) and 23½in (60cm) tall with narrow, short leaves that grow in pairs directly opposite one another. The leaves have a central white midrib. In itself, this plant is an attractive addition to a garden, because it looks human-made. It would work well growing out of a low ground cover in many different garden scenarios—urban, tropical, and cottage. Like a lot of weeds in this chapter, *Euphorbia lathyris* is a woodland-edge plant and therefore tolerates shade, but will grow larger with an hour or two of direct sunlight or dappled light each day.

In its second year the plant races skyward in spring, at which point it can branch, but remains bolt upright, beginning to flower from mid-spring until early summer. Its flowers are a very subtle shade of the typical *Euphorbia* acid green and form in a large, unusual triangular shape that is set against the dark leaves with white highlights. In its final form *Euphorbia lathyris* reminds me of a geometric shape in a kaleidoscope.

Did you know?
Euphorbia sap, a white latex, is phototoxic, reacting to sunlight to cause skin blisters. By way of example, I once came up in huge, horrible but painless blisters all over my left ear after transplanting *Euphorbia lathyris* into our garden. I must have brushed some sap against my ear. Always handle *Euphorbia lathyris* with care—and gloves. Avoid coming into contact with the sap and especially avoid getting in your eyes. Wash it out if you do and go straight to the emergency room. It's mildly toxic if eaten—don't eat the seed pods, even though they look like capers (giving the plant the common name, caper spurge).

Bringing *Euphorbia lathyris* into your garden
You can transplant *Euphorbia lathyris* in its second year while flowering, but it's undeniably better to do so when the plants are first-year seedlings. And the smaller, the better. If you see a flowering plant in the wild, keep an eye on its developing seed pods. Once they are ripe you have to be quick to catch the seeds, because—like many weeds—the seed pods are explosive, catapulting their contents over a significant distance. Each pod contains three fairly large seeds. Take all three and throw them in the garden where you'd like the plant to grow. Germination can take a while—up to a year—so don't give up.

The overall habit of the plant, with its narrow upright form and unique coloring, makes it a captivating addition to any sunny or part-shade garden bed. You can group it together, but, really, it's best treated like a statue and dotted through a garden bed of lower plants or ground cover, allowing it to shine as a feature. The combination of *Euphorbia lathyris* and *Beta vulgaris* subsp. *cicla*, with its lightning-bolt red stems, is out of this world.

Invasiveness
Each plant produces a reasonable number of seeds and scatters them all over the place, but invasiveness is a strong word for *Euphorbia lathyris*. Promiscuous is probably more appropriate—it will reproduce in large enough numbers to be mildly annoying, but not enough to outcompete anything else.

Control
Removing the flowers is the only way to stop the seeds from scattering themselves around, because the flowers, and therefore seeds, gradually appear over a fairly long period of time. Removing the obvious seedlings as you see them is the best method of control once plants are in place. Do wear gardening gloves to avoid the sap getting onto your hands.

Cultivated varieties
Naturally occurring in the UK, *Euphorbia amygdaloides* var. *robbiae* has become a popular garden variety with darker green leaves.

Herb robert

Geranium robertianum

Geranium robertianum is a beautiful plant—its fern-like foliage providing the main draw and being the first thing you're likely to notice. A garden full of it would be an ethereal sight, which is just as well, because it can take over.

Care: 1/5

Effort: 2/5

Rebelliousness: 4/5

Plant family: Geraniaceae

Max size: 19½in (50cm) tall, 19½in (50cm) wide

Color: pink

Flowers: May–October

Pot friendly: yes

Soil: any, even dry

Situation: shade, part shade

Range: Europe, North America (USDA hardiness zones 5–9)

Origin: Europe, Asia, northern Africa

Compared with cultivated geraniums, *Geranium robertianum* is gifted the finest, most delicate green leaves, each tinted red, especially on the petiole. Allowed to grow large or massed together, the layers of fine leaves create a lovely green, hazy fuzz. The small, light pink flowers stand out brightly in shade. Appearing all summer long, the flowers are fairly sparse—which is an asset rather than a liability, because it allows the leaves and flowers to work together. Don't rub the leaves, however, because they produce a subtle, unpleasant smell.

Owing to its fondness for shade and its unobtrusive root system, *Geranium robertianum* is perfectly suited to being left to its own devices beneath established large perennials, shrubs, and trees— an understory that causes no problems.

Bringing *Geranium robertianum* into your garden
It's highly likely that *Geranium robertianum* is already in your garden—try transplanting a small seedling by digging up as much soil around the root ball as you can, without damaging the roots. Or, regularly check on larger plants until their flowers form seed pods. Explode them into a paper bag and scatter seeds around where you'd like them to grow.

As few grasses grow in shady garden beds, particularly fluffy-flowering types, *Geranium robertianum* can do the job of softening combinations of other plants, albeit without also giving vertical shape to a bed. Grown next to large-leaved *Hosta*, *Brunnera macrophylla*, or weedy *Arum maculatum*, *Heuchera*, *Asplenium scolopendrium* (see p.116) or *Euphorbia amygdaloides*, *Geranium robertianum* adds contrasting leaf form against the bolder leaves.

Geranium robertianum looks particularly beautiful grown in combination with *Lamium album* (see p.98), which offers loose spires, while *Geranium robertianum* tumbles and scrambles around. The white and light pink of the two flowers works well together, too.

Try growing *Geranium robertianum* among *Hyacinthoides non-scripta* (see p.22) for a lovely blue-and-pink pastel combo in spring.

Invasiveness
Geranium robertianum is highly invasive in a "herd of teddy bears"-kind of way. It will grow everywhere and anywhere, but is easy to keep under control. Although *Geranium robertianum* likes shade, it will grow in sun, too.

Control
While herbicides will work well on *Geranium robertianum*, using them as a means of control is a pointless exercise because seeds in the soil will soon grow back. The best method of control is to remove unwanted plants by hand or to hoe. To remove by hand, grip as many leaves near the central crown as you can and tug—the plant should come away easily, because the roots are weak. If not, dig a little with a trowel to loosen the soil first.

Cultivated varieties
Geranium robertianum "Album" has white flowers making for a very fine plant indeed—although it's still as invasive. "Celtic White" is pure white on green leaves, is smaller, and is less invasive. Both are available online.

Stinking iris

Iris foetidissima

Not all flowers need to be bright attention grabbers, some can draw you in with slow-burning beauty the color of Milky Way mists. *Iris foetidissima* is one of Europe's native irises and, like many native woodland plants, has an ethereal feel when in flower, thanks to the mixture of color on the large petals.

Care: 1/5

Effort: 2/5

Rebelliousness: 1/5

Plant family: Iridaceae

Max size: 27½in (70cm) tall, 12in (30cm) wide

Color: purple-brown to yellow and blue

Flowers: June–July

Pot friendly: yes

Soil: any, even very dry

Situation: sun to part shade

Range: Europe, northern Africa, North America (USDA hardiness zones 6–9), Australasia

Origin: Europe, northern Africa

The strengths of this plant are three-fold.

First, and most importantly, its sword-shaped leaves, typical of irises, make an excellent addition to shady garden beds. It provides a strong shape—in the form of vertical spikes—that contrasts well with softer leaves, such as those of *Meconopsis cambrica* (see p.100), and it rises through the ground cover of plants such as *Pachysandra terminalis* and *Asarum europaeum*.

Second, when in flower, the subtle and varied coloring of its petals draw people close to examine the markings. No two *Iris foetidissima* flowers are alike—they range from cosmic browns and purples, to jewel-like lighter yellows and blues. All the petals tend to have unusual marks and patterns. Scattered around a shade garden bed, the flowers won't have impact from afar, but the feel they lend to the space is invaluable.

Finally, after flowering, the seed pods will burst open to reveal bright orange or red fruits. If you plan it carefully, you can time these to coordinate with flowers and other berries, such as those of the *Pyracantha*.

Did you know?
The specific epithet *foetidissima* means "smell," resulting in the plant's common name, stinking iris. Rub its leaves and you will notice an unusual smell of beef.

Bringing *Iris foetidissima* into your garden
Where it is found widely growing in empty lots, you could take a small plant and transfer it—although it is considered a wildflower in the UK, so you mustn't dig it up from wild spots, such as nature reserves and woodlands. A better solution is to look for the fruits when ripe and knock off some of these into a bag to take home and scatter around the garden—crush the berries when you do so.

Invasiveness
This plant is fairly invasive, especially outside its native range. It is happy growing in sun and shade, and in dry as well as wet conditions. This means *Iris foetidissima* is fast to build strong clumps and then spread seed around. Fairly hard to get rid of once established, it will grow back from pieces of rhizome.

Control
Dig out large clumps being sure to check a few weeks later for regrowth from missed pieces of root. Cut off flower heads once they are finished to avoid the plant producing seeds.

Cultivated varieties
Iris foetidissima var. *citrina* is a naturally occurring—rather than cultivated—form of the plant with lighter petals, thanks to more shades of yellow.

White deadnettle

Lamium album

Easily dismissed as a stinging nettle, *Lamium album* is far more refined than the common nettle (*Urtica dioica*) and is the potential star of a shady garden bed. It has beautiful, incredibly long-lasting whorls of white flowers that appear around its stems from as early as April all the way through to November and December.

Care: 2/5	
Effort: 3/5	
Rebelliousness: 4/5	

Plant family: Lamiaceae

Max size: 9½in (50cm) tall, 15½in (40cm) wide

Color: pure white

Flowers: April–November

Pot friendly: yes

Soil: any

Situation: part shade

Range: global (USDA zones unknown)

Origin: Europe, Russia, Asia

Found in some parts of New England, it's important to say that *Lamium album* doesn't sting, leading to the common name, deadnettle. The white flowers are the clue that this is a plant that's perfectly safe to touch. (*Urtica dioica* is a larger, coarser plant with green tassels for flowers.)

Although each flower is quite small and often slightly obscured by *Lamium album*'s leaves, the clusters of pure white hold their color for a long time and positively glow in a shady spot. As the year progresses, the plant produces more and more whorls until the white flowers are numerous. They make beautiful cut flowers for a vase.

Usually you'll find *Lamium album* growing in scruffy waste areas where it is not shown to its best. Planted in a shady garden bed, however, either as a clump or a number of clumps dotted throughout, it is quite an upright grower with good shape and lush, green leaves (remove any tatty, wayward growth to keep it smart).

Did you know?
Lamium album is edible, including the flowers—try adding them to salads or desserts, or suck out the sweet nectar. Eat the younger leaves rather than the older ones.

Bringing *Lamium album* into your garden
The easiest way to acquire a plant is to dig it up when you find it and then replant it in your garden, in your designated spot.

To avoid people thinking you've let stinging nettles into your beds, grow it with plants that complement it. For example, growing it among other white flowering plants, such as white *Digitalis* (see p.21), white *Aquilegia vulgaris*, *Brunnera macrophylla* "Mr Morse" (with its equally beautiful silvery-white, large leaves), and some lush, green ferns for contrast, demonstrates intention, as well as looking exceptionally beautiful. Growing it beneath the white trunks of *Betula utilis* var. *jacquemontii* would set off the whole display. Position some white furniture nearby and you could have created a modern version of the famous Sissinghurst white garden.

Of course, *Lamium album* also goes well with pastel plants, such as the pale pink flowers of *Geranium robertianum* (see p.94) and *Hyacinthoides non-scripta* (see p.22).

Invasiveness
Like its relatives *Monarda* and *Mentha*, *Lamium album* will spread by seed, as well as by rhizomes that grow just under or at the surface of the soil, with new shoots popping up along them. Left unchecked, *Lamium album* can spread quite quickly, although not as aggressively as *Mentha*.

Control
Pull out spreading rhizomes occasionally. Dig up large groups and replant the plants in smaller numbers. If necessary, plant in a large pot or surrounded by a Butyl rubber barrier (see p.43) to stop the rhizomes spreading.

Cultivated varieties
There are no cultivated varieties, although there is another species called *Lamium purpureum*. This is very similar, but it is smaller with purple-ish new leaves, and flowers that range from pale to bright pink.

Welsh poppy

Meconopsis cambrica

Bright yellow and orange flowers are usually found in hot or tropical sunny garden beds rather than shade, but this easy-to-grow poppy will bring high-impact, bold color even to the shadiest spot.

Care: 1/5

Effort: 2/5

Rebelliousness: 3/5

Plant family: Papaveraceae

Max size: 19½in (50cm) tall, 19½in (50cm) wide

Color: yellow or orange

Flowers: June–July

Pot friendly: yes

Soil: any damp

Situation: shade, part shade

Range: Europe, North America (USDA hardiness zones 3–11), New Zealand

Origin: western Europe

Buck the (admittedly beautiful) trend of using white and pastels in shade: instead, use standout bold, yellow flowers of the woodland plant *Meconopsis cambrica*. Occasionally, you might find orange-flowered variants, although these are rarer and will often revert to yellow over time (unless you quickly remove the yellows). Like white flowers, bold yellow and orange petals will glow like jewels against a darker backdrop.

Closely associated with Wales, *Meconopsis cambrica* is native to the rest of the UK and to western Europe, too. It is the only native European poppy in the genus *Meconopsis*.

Bringing *Meconopsis cambrica* into your garden

The best way to introduce *Meconopsis cambrica* is to plant it from seeds you've collected. When poppy seed is ready to collect, you'll see gaps at the top of the seed head. This allows you to tap seeds out into a paper bag. If you want orange poppies, you must collect seed from a plant you know to have orange flowers. (Keep an eye out for yellow-flowered plants and remove them immediately to avoid cross-pollination with the orange ones.)

Garden designers often use repetition to draw the eye along garden beds and views. This can come to an abrupt halt when part of a sunny garden bed falls into shade and vice-versa. However, careful selection of different species of plant with the same colors and sizes allows you to blend garden beds and keep the repetition going further. For example, in the shady side of the garden bed, grow groups of *Meconopsis cambrica*, and on the sunny side grow *Calendula*, *Solidago rigida*, or other sun-loving yellow poppies. Although their differences are noticeable when you see them side-by-side, from a distance people will simply see the repeated splashes of color.

Try using *Meconopsis cambrica* to continue the theme of a tropical garden into shady corners. Grow them among *Hakonechloa*, *Heuchera* and ferns (especially *Dryopteris erythrosora*, which has orange-tinted new fronds). The ferny foliage of *Meconopsis cambrica* works well alongside the leaves of *Helleborus* and *Hosta*. In constantly damp soil, grow *Meconopsis cambrica* alongside brightly colored *Primula candelabra*, the orange looking particularly good with hot pink; the yellow with purple. Both look good with other yellow, orange and red flowers.

Invasiveness

Meconopsis cambrica will seed itself around, but it isn't particularly invasive.

Control

Pull out plants as you spot them; or cut off seed heads before they ripen to control numbers and reduce spread.

Cultivated varieties

Not a cultivar, but a naturally occurring variant, *Meconopsis cambrica* var. *aurantiacum* has deep, orange flowers, which sometimes have twice the number of petals per flower.

Chapter 5

Weeds for Rich, Damp Soils

Permanently damp soils can be as problematic as very dry soils. Damp soil occurs where water can't drain away effectively— think ditches and dips, the foot of a hill, river banks, or in areas where there is a natural underground spring. You can go to great expense adding drainage to dry out waterlogged soils, but in fact they offer an opportunity to grow plants that are adapted for life in the wet. Some weeds love damp soils—let them tempt you to add to lush and colorful displays to your garden.

Wild chervil

Anthriscus sylvestris

Anthriscus sylvestris is one of those plants that happily jumps the barrier between classic and contemporary. It has lush, ferny green leaves and, in spring, airy, clean-cut white flowers held high on thin stems.

Care: 2/5

Effort: 3/5

Rebelliousness: 3/5

☠

Plant family: Apiaceae

Max size: 59in (150cm) tall, 19½in (50cm) wide

Color: white

Flowers: May–June

Pot friendly: yes

Soil: any

Situation: sun to part shade

Range: global (USDA hardiness zones 7–10)

Origin: Eurasia, Africa

In late winter, as *Anthriscus sylvestris*'s beautiful leaves begin to emerge, looking particularly effective with *Galanthus* spp. and *Lamium album* (see p.98), we know that the new year has begun. Then, as soon as spring breaks, it grows rapidly until its umbels of white flowers, held high on thin stems, emerge in mid-spring, telling us that winter is a distant memory.

Although *Anthriscus sylvestris* likes constant moisture, it doesn't like to be waterlogged. Its preferred conditions are on the edges of dank woods and in hedges with part shade. Grow it in damp soils, but in spots where the ground will receive some drainage, such as part way up a slope or bank, or on the edges of a damp hollow. *Anthriscus sylvestris* is a good cut flower. However, be warned: old tales claim that bringing this plant into the house could cause someone to die, giving it its lesser-known name of Mother Die.

Bringing *Anthriscus sylvestris* into your garden

Anthriscus sylvestris forms a deep taproot, so it doesn't like root disturbance. For this reason seeds are the best option. Revisit a clump a couple of months after flowering and you'll find dark seeds in place of the flowers. Hold a paper bag underneath and tap the seeds into it.

Sow the seeds as soon as you can by scattering them on bare soil. They prefer a few months of stratification, a period of cold to break their dormancy. You'll soon spot the leaves when they germinate (although it is best to mark where you sowed, because it's easy to forget). The small plants will grow leaves in the first year, and flower from the second, making fall a good time for sowing, ready for a flower-filled spring.

Large areas of *Anthriscus sylvestris* in flower can be quite breathtaking, providing a delicate veil of white. Often this is the only tall plant in flower at this time of the year, and worth growing near late-blossomed apple or cherry trees. *Anthriscus sylvestris* and white *Digitalis purpurea* (see p.21) in combination can look particularly beautiful, although they may flower at slightly different times, depending on the weather. Planting topiary in the middle of a swathe of *Anthriscus sylvestris* will enable each to set off the other in a spectacular way: the solid, dark form of the topiary contrasting with the light tapestry of *Anthriscus sylvestris*.

When you're thinking about the structural design of your garden, use *Anthriscus sylvestris* with white furniture and gray paving slabs for a truly designer look. Try sawn stone for something contemporary.

Invasiveness

The main method of spread is by seed, and *Anthriscus sylvestris* does produce a lot. It's not particularly hard to keep the plant under

control, but once established it will keep trying to take over. It is considered a noxious weed in Massachusetts and Washington.

Control

Cut off flowers when they've one finished and before the seeds ripen. Remove plants by forking out the taproot to eradicate the plant completely. Seeds don't last particularly long in the soil, so over a few years of repeated forking out, you can have the plant under control.

Cultivated varieties

Anthriscus sylvestris "Ravenswing" has black foliage, giving its name.

Giant hogweed

Heracleum mantegazzianum

Grown sensibly and handled carefully, *Heracleum mantegazzianum* is a beautiful and exotic plant, which is why the Victorians introduced it to our gardens. Its star attraction is its huge, 23½in-wide (60cm) umbels of white flowers held on towering stems with equally striking leaves.

Care: 1/5

Effort: 4/5

Rebelliousness: 3/5

Plant family: Apiaceae

Max size: 15 feet (5m) tall, 6 feet (2m) wide

Color: white

Flowers: June–August

Pot friendly: no

Soil: rich, damp

Situation: full sun

Range: Europe, western Asia, North America (USDA zones unknown), Iceland, Australasia

Origin: Caucasus mountains, central Eurasia

To power such enormous growth, *Heracleum mantegazzianum* requires rich, damp soil in full sun. Working well in large landscapes, at the back of a garden bed or as an exotic curiosity in smaller gardens, and with everything from tropical to urban styles, it is a showstopper.

To say *Heracleum mantegazzianum* has a bad reputation is an understatement. It's considered an invasive weed in most countries and many fear its sap. Toward the end of the twentieth century, there was a storm of negative publicity for this poor weed: stories of children being rushed to hospital with blisters and burns; people in space suits dispatched to eradicate this toxic terror.

In reality, people had been growing *Heracleum mantegazzianum* for more than 150 years, knowing full well its phototoxic sap can cause extreme skin sensitivity in sunlight. We just need to be aware and to educate children, in particular, to stay clear.

If sap does come into contact with your skin, it's not the end of the world, just make sure you rinse the area thoroughly as soon as possible. You would need a lot of sap and a reasonable exposure to full sun to receive severe burns.

Bringing *Heracleum mantegazzianum* into your garden

In the US *Heracleum mantegazzianum* is outlawed, so it cannot be grown in gardens. However, if you ever do come across it, take a moment to enjoy its beauty as a plant.

In other countries, in terms of design, think of it as a temporary tree. The scale of its flower heads immediately makes it the focal point of any palette. If you have it growing in your garden, try planting a group of smaller perennials or annuals in front. In the past it would have been repeated down garden beds, drawing along the eye. Being monocarpic, it will grow leaves for a few years before flowering once and then dying.

Surrounded by other giants such as *Gunnera manicata*, *Tetrapanax papyrifer* "Rex," and *Musa basjoo*, *Heracleum mantegazzianum* will be well contained and make even the biggest person feel tiny.

Invasiveness

This is only an invasive plant when not controlled. Its means of spread is by seed. If the seeds land in rivers or streams, the flow will carry them downstream to other banks.

Control

If growing *Heracleum mantegazzianum* in other parts of the world, find a sheltered spot, such as damp soil surrounded by hedges, walls

or other plants, and well away from water. Seeds will travel around the garden, but not that far from the plant. To reduce numbers, cut off the flowerheads before it seeds or, to remove the plant entirely, simply dig it out, including its taproot, and burn or compost.

Cultivated varieties

None known.

Purple loosestrife

Lythrum salicaria

Flowering in mid- to late-summer, *Lythrum salicaria* brings tall, bold, vertical, pink–purple spikes long after *Digitalis purpurea* (see p.21) and other early summer flowers have finished.

Care: 2/5

Effort: 3/5

Rebelliousness: 4/5

☠

Plant family: Lythraceae

Max size: 6 feet (2m) tall, 19½ in (50cm) wide

Color: pink–purple

Flowers: June–August

Pot friendly: no

Soil: any permanently damp

Situation: full sun

Range: global (USDA hardiness zones 4–9)

Origin: Europe, northern Africa, Asia

Usually found along the banks of waterways and rivers, reveling in the waterlogged conditions, *Lythrum salicaria* can grow happily in any damp soil that doesn't dry out. In damp ground away from water, it will be easier to control.

It's such an easy plant to grow (despite its height you won't need to fertilize or support the plant), producing excellent flowers every year. Pinching out the main shoots in spring will cause the plant to branch, producing a greater number of shorter flower spikes. This can be useful in some situations, but the appeal of the plant is usually its tall, vertical spikes.

Bringing *Lythrum salicaria* into your garden
Grow the plant from seed collected in late summer and sprinkle where you want it. It's a vigorous grower and shouldn't need much more effort to grow than this. You can grow in pots initially.

Although traditionally considered a cottage garden plant, *Lythrum salicaria* has a strong color that helps it fit easily into modern and tropical gardens. Alongside foliage plants such as *Canna*, *Cyperus involucratus*, and the giant rhubarb relative, *Gunnera manicata*, *Lythrum salicaria* can contribute well to exoticism. You'll achieve a gloriously colorful display growing it in a damp garden bed alongside shorter plants, such as colorful *Primula bulleyana* and the reds, pinks, and whites of *Sanguisorba*. The rigid vertical shape and strong color bring drama to the back of a garden bed, creating a beautiful focal point. *Monarda didyma* enjoys similar, albeit not waterlogged, conditions and the more domed habit of the plant with its whorls of flowers contrasts nicely in shape. For shocking contrast, try *Rudbeckia fulgida*, too.

Invasiveness
In permanently wet areas *Lythrum salicaria* will self-seed quickly (plants produce upward of two million seeds a year) and spread, but it's never so invasive in its native habitat of Europe and Asia as to overtake all other plants. In gardens rather than river banks, where things are a tad drier and there is more competition, it's much better behaved.

In the USA, however, *Lythrum salicaria* is currently considered a noxious weed and gardeners are permitted to plant only the sterile cultivars. Evidence shows these can still produce seed when cross-pollinated with wild plants. The plant's invasiveness in the US is owing to the lack of bugs that treat it as food—back in Europe the mini-beasts keep it under control. Native alternatives that grow iin similar conditions include *Eutrochium maculatum*, *Asclepias incarnata*, or *Monarda* varieties.

Control
Lythrum salicaria spreads predominantly by seed. Cut off flower pikes when they're finished and before they can fully set seed.

Or, to eradicate plants entirely, cut them down before they flower and pull them out if there are too many. You'll need to use a garden fork to lever out the large, woody rootstocks of established plants, being sure to remove every root. Burn the plants, rather than composting, otherwise seeds and roots can survive. Repeat for a few years.

Cultivated varieties
"Blush" has light pink flowers.

Baby's tears

Soleirolia soleirolii

Soleirolia soleirolii will form a luxurious green carpet in your garden as it grows. With tiny, barely visible flowers, it is the perfect green backdrop for your garden beds— though watch out, it spreads quickly! It's a member of the nettle family, *Urticaceae*, but it doesn't sting.

Care: 1/5

Effort: 5/5

Rebelliousness: 5/5

Plant family: Urticaceae

Max size: 4in (10cm) tall, 39½in (100cm) wide

Color: green

Flowers: summer, but not visible

Pot friendly: yes

Soil: any permanently damp

Situation: shade, part shade

Range: global (USDA hardiness zones 9–11)

Origin: western central Mediterranean

Soleirolia soleirolii is a very low-growing plant that forms a carpet of tiny, round, shiny leaves. It's like moss with much less trouble. Spreading quickly, it can add a rich, green covering to garden beds, around ponds, and in-between paths and slabs. In this respect its usefulness for adding a green backdrop to a garden is second to none. Late-Victorians introduced *Soleirolia soleirolii* from its native Italy, but when people realized how uncontrollable it was, they quickly beat a hasty retreat and avoided adding it to their gardens.

Purely ornamental, you can't walk on *Soleirolia soleirolii* without crushing it, so it's not a practical replacement for a busy lawn. Its white flowers are so tiny you're unlikely ever to see them. One of the best uses I've seen is in a private garden in South London (see opposite). The owner used the plant beneath a small forest of tree ferns, making the garden glow emerald green when looking at it from inside their corten steel extension.

Bringing *Soleirolia soleirolii* into your garden
If you know a patch of this plant, just dig out a small piece, with some roots, and replant it, giving it a good soak. A few weeks later, you'll notice how quickly it grows! Alternatively, it's sold widely as a house plant in nurseries and florists.

It's most suitable for foliage and jungly gardens, where green is the main color, as well as Japanese-style gardens, where you can use it in place of moss. In winter it's likely to die back, except in mild locations, but will return when temperatures rise in spring.

If you prefer you can grow it indoors, as a houseplant in a pot, where you need to ensure the soil never dries out. The plant wilts when dry, giving the clue to water it. However, waiting for the wilt is a risky game because a day too late and the plant will be dead. Growing the plant inside will help you contain it—but the strategy is not foolproof: I kept mine indoors in a terrarium and somehow it made the leap past the 15½ in (40cm) house wall and into our garden—perhaps through a tiny fragment of plant on my clothes.

Invasiveness
Many gardeners love the look of *Soleirolia soleirolii* but fear rightly its ruthless spread.

Control
Although it copes well with shade, *Soleirolia soleirolii* does need some light, which means dense planting will slow its spread. Using it in pots (or in solid, restricted garden beds) so it runs out of soil to root in will contain it up to a point. Weed killer is pointless in an established garden, because you can't avoid other plants, so hand weeding is the

only way to remove unwanted clumps. Luckily it rips out easily, even if it's likely to grow back from remaining fragments.

Cultivated varieties
Soleirolia soleirolii is available in different shades of green, from silver and dark green to lime. The various shades look good mixed together inside, but it's probably better in the garden to opt for a single color to prevent things looking fussy.

Common michaelmas daisy

Symphyotrichum x salignum

Symphyotrichum x *salignum* will grow in all kinds of conditions from dry shade to damp sun. The plant's flowers can come in a variety of colors from white, pink, and purple to the more common blues. They provide a much-needed, late-season blast of flowers leading into and all through fall.

Care: 2/5

Effort: 3/5

Rebelliousness: 3/5

Plant family: Asteraceae

Max size: 59in (150cm) tall, 19½in (50cm) wide

Color: pale blue to mauve

Flowers: July–October

Pot friendly: yes

Soil: any permanently damp

Situation: full sun

Range: global (USDA zones unknown)

Origin: Europe, from North American parents

This entry is a celebration of all the North American asters. Now common around the world, these plants have pale blue to mauve flowers that have become easy to overlook. There are now many species and hybrids—here I'll talk about *Symphyotrichum* x *salignum*, but really this entry refers to any aster you might find.

Most asters come from North America and have overrun the rest of the world with their weedy ways. *Symphyotrichum* x *salignum* is interesting because it didn't originate in North America—instead it's a crossbreed of *Symphyotrichum novi-belgii* and *Symphyotrichum lanceolatum*, which did. The hybrid, though, occurred in Europe at some point and now grows everywhere it can find damp soil, from ditches and river banks to front gardens, medians, and claggy, city walls.

Between knee and waist high, these are strong plants that afford enough airiness to mingle happily in a garden bed. Their long-lasting small daisies begin appearing in mid-summer and continue until there is frost—the lighter flowers are very welcome in the slowly darkening days. Allowed to grow as weeds, they can look a tad messy, but grown purposefully with other plants, they're transformed, adding a lightness of color and of touch.

Bringing *Symphyotrichum x salignum* into your garden
The easiest way to obtain *Symphyotrichum* x *salignum* is to dig up a plant, taking as much root ball as possible. I would plant it in the garden when it is in flower, so you can choose the exact shade of petals you want—flower color can vary a lot. Alternatively, select the plant in fall, tying a little yarn around it to help you find it again, and then transplant in spring.

To grow from seed, pinch off the seeds in fall when the flowers are going over—the seeds should come away easily if they're ready. Then sprinkle them where you would like the plant to grow.

Symphyotrichum x *salignum* combines well with other, lighter, pastel colors. One of my favorite plant combinations of all time, however, is the pale blue aster against a contrasting hot pink or magenta from *Nerine bowdenii* (in a pot as it likes good drainage) or a *Dahlia*, such as "Winston Churchill" or "Hillcrest Royal." With fall sun these flowers appear all the richer and more beautiful, offering precious color that shines brightly on the cusp of winter. The contrast highlights the larger flowers' interesting shape. Asters also combine well with spikes of *Lythrum salicaria* (see p.108) or *Persicaria*, which both like similar conditions.

Invasiveness
Although *Symphyotrichum* x *salignum* will multiply from seed easily, and you might often see it in large groups along railroads and other

vacant spaces, it's not that invasive. It will multiply, but usually not at the expense of other plants.

Control
Simply pull it out as soon as possible when you see it growing.

Cultivated varieties
There are many cultivated varieties of aster available to buy and you'll find various different species growing wild.

Chapter 6

Weeds for Containers, Pots, and Window Boxes

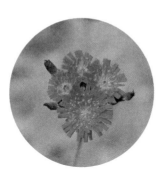

Containers make the perfect homes for many different weeds, drawing attention to and enhancing their beautiful shapes and colors. Growing weeds in pots restricts their spread, allowing you to grow more vigorous plants than you'd want to let loose in the ground. Pots also mean you can move your weeds around for different effects. This chapter highlights a number of weeds well-suited to pot life, but feel free to experiment if your favorites don't feature.

Hart's tongue fern

Asplenium scolopendrium

Many ferns enjoy life in a pot and *Asplenium scolopendrium*, commonly found growing out of walls as well as the ground across the Northern Hemisphere, is no exception. It works particularly well in shade. The fronds resemble the shape of a deer's tongue, giving the plant its common name.

Care: 2/5

Effort: 1/5

Rebelliousness: 2/5

Plant family: Aspleniaceae

Max size: 23½in (60cm) tall and 23½in (60cm) wide

Color: green

Flowers: none

Pot friendly: yes

Soil: damp to dry, preferably alkaline

Situation: shade, part shade

Range: Northern Hemisphere (USDA hardiness zones 5—9)

Origin: Europe, northern Africa, Asia

Unusually for a fern, *Asplenium scolopendrium*'s fronds are undivided, emerging from a central crown in a green shuttlecock. The main appeal is the way in which the solid fronds, grown against other leaf shapes (even different ferns), create a pleasing contrast of form. As a shade-loving fern, *Asplenium scolopendrium* brings bright, lush green to darker spots in the garden.

Asplenium scolopendrium will suit any garden—from country dwelling to urban patio. In fact, city gardens are a particularly good fit, while no foliage or tropical garden is complete without one.

Toward the end of winter, you'll notice the new fronds in the center of the plant begin to swell and slowly unravel. Snip off the old fronds as soon as you see this happen, being careful not to damage the vulnerable new ones. Although short-lived, these few weeks as the fronds unfurl make for an exciting foliage display as spectacular as any flower.

A top tip is that the size of the fronds generally comes down to levels of moisture and nutrients in the soil. Grown in consistently damp, fresh, peat-free compost, the fronds will be large and luxurious. Allowed to grow in drier conditions, the fronds will be shorter. Either is fine—it depends what look you are going for.

Bringing *Asplenium scolopendrium* into your garden

Look on shady, damp walls and you'll be sure to find some *Asplenium scolopendrium*. Lever out a small plant from the wall, being very careful to save the fragile roots. Pot up the plant in damp compost. Generally it prefers growing in slightly alkaline conditions (lime and mortar walls are a natural home), but really it will grow in any soil.

I find *Asplenium scolopendrium* looks best growing in a tall, narrow, almost vase-shaped container, where the fronds appear to be spraying out of the top like a fountain. It looks great in traditional terracotta pots, as well as more modern charcoal gray.

Invasiveness

The native variety, *Asplenium scolopendrium var. americanum* is threatened across the whole of America and endangered in New York, Tennessee, and Michigan.

Control

Easy: remove plants by hand as you spot them.

Cultivated varieties

There are many cultivated varieties with different-shaped fronds. "Cristatum Group" divides at the end of the frond creating crests, while "Crispum Group" has wavy, crimped edges.

English daisy

Bellis perennis

It's easy to overlook something as common as *Bellis perennis*, the English daisy. Examine closely, though, and this tiny, evergreen plant's many flowers make a bright, immaculately formed addition to the garden that is worthy of celebration.

Care: 0/5

Effort: 2/5

Rebelliousness: 5/5

Plant family: Asteraceae

Max size: 4in (10cm) tall, limitless spread

Color: white petals with a yellow center

Flowers: all year

Pot friendly: yes

Soil: any

Situation: full sun, part shade

Range: Europe, North America (USDA hardiness zones 4–8) and South America, Australia, Asia

Origin: Europe

Masses of *Bellis perennis* in lawns can be a happy sight, conjuring memories of making daisy chains as a child. In that vein *Bellis perennis* lends itself to shabby chic or a romantic vibe—try terracotta pots, stone urns, and pots that are painted or glazed. Don't worry about the odd chip or crack, which only adds to the look. Raising the flowers high up in their pots, shines new light on this common little flower.

Any growing medium—such as peat-free compost—will do, but as they establish themselves keep the plants well-watered. Once established, though, they cope well with drought—which is just as well, because it's easy to forget to water pots and the soil can dry out quickly on warm days. Remove the flowers as they finish and the plant will quickly produce more.

Position a pot of *Bellis perennis* as a centerpiece on a table, on steps or even in window boxes. It will immediately invoke feelings of freedom and carefree sunny days. Grow enough to make your own daisy chain headwear—homegrown fun for small children and big children wanting to rock the ethereal look. The young leaves of *Bellis perennis* are edible and great for salads, getting tougher with age.

Did you know?
Like all plants in the Asteraceae plant family—such as the American prairie flowers *Echinacea*, *Rudbeckia*, and *Helianthus*—the daisy's flower heads are actually formed from thousands of minuscule flowers in the tiny central yellow disk. What we know as the white petals, which are called florets, are there to attract and guide pollinating insects—they are not real petals at all. And, although these days we often play the game "loves me, loves me not" with those *Bellis perennis* florets, it's traditionally played using *Leucanthemum vulgare* (see p.84), the larger ox-eye daisy.

Bringing *Bellis perennis* into your garden
If you don't already have *Bellis perennis* in your garden congratulations on witnessing a minor miracle, so common is this plant. To add it to a pot, simply dig up a small clump, being careful not to damage the roots. Plant it into a pot about 1–2in (3–5cm) wider than the plant itself, because it will grow reasonably quickly throughout the year.

Bellis perennis mixes well in a larger pot with other relatively small plants, preferably of complementary colors, such as yellow and white, and contrasting shapes. Try *Taraxacum officinale*, white *Achillea millefolium* and a low-growing grass, such as *Festuca amethystina*, creating a meadowy look in a pot. Or, grow your *Bellis perennis* with a white version of *Armeria maritima*; and dwarf daffodils such as *Narcissus bulbocodium* for a very beautiful, long-lasting plant

combination. Light purple or mauve flowers, such as those found on *Thymus vulgaris*, also work because they provide the color-wheel opposite yellow, giving perfect contrast; and white goes with everything.

Invasiveness
Bellis perennis is considered invasive because it spreads so quickly (mainly by seeds), especially in lawns where it thrives in the short grass. In the US it's an introduced, invasive species.

Control
Remove the dead flowers, which will prevent the plant producing seeds that then jump from the pot. Plus, deadheading will encourage more flowers to grow. In a garden, dig out the plants by hand.

Cultivated varieties
So easy and loved a plant, *Bellis perennis* is much-cultivated. The "Tasso Series" is well known for its double flowers (that is, lots of rays that together create a pom-pom) and range of colors. There are many other cultivars.

Jupiter's beard

Centranthus ruber

Centranthus ruber is one of those plants you see everywhere: in abandoned front yards, footpaths and parking lots, on railroads, even up walls. "I know it's a weed, but I've always loved the flowers," my mother once said of it. I had to agree, *Centranthus ruber* is a beautiful plant. And it's easily grown in pots.

Care: 0/5

Effort: 3/5

Rebelliousness: 3/5

Plant family: Caprifoliaceae

Max size: 39½in (100cm) tall, 19½in (50cm) wide

Color: red, dull pink, and white

Flowers: May–October

Pot friendly: yes

Soil: dry, nutrient poor

Situation: sun to part shade

Range: Europe, America (USDA hardiness zones 4–9), Africa, Australasia

Origin: Mediterranean

Centranthus ruber is a widespread garden escapee, originally added to garden beds from its natural Mediterranean habitat, and now on the run all across the Europe. In the US the plant prefers the slightly cooler summers of northern states, although it does very well in hot California summers too. This ubiquitous nature means that we easily overlook it, having long forgotten the attributes that made us fall in love with it in the first place.

Forming a knee-high plant, the leaves and stems are a light minty green, with a hint of gray. Flowers—in pink, magenta, crimson, and white (and all shades in between)—form a profusion of colorful tufts from spring until fall. That long flowering period is one of the plant's greatest characteristics. Furthermore, lots of pollinating insects love *Centranthus ruber*, making it great for attracting butterflies, bees, and the slightly rarer, ultra-cool hummingbird hawk moth.

Bringing *Centranthus ruber* into your garden

You can buy *Centranthus ruber* online, but it's more fun to go on the hunt for a wild plant to bring home. Throughout summer keep your eyes peeled, paying close attention to the great differences in flower color. When you've found the shade you want, look around the larger plant for a young, smaller one. Dig this up without damaging roots and take it home.

The variety of color and the plant's shape make *Centranthus ruber* wonderfully versatile and easy to place in any garden. Traditionally considered a plant best-suited to cottage gardens, where it still works well, the white *Centranthus ruber* "Albus" will nonetheless fit perfectly in a sleek, modern or urban space. Gravel gardens suit all colors; while the rich magenta and crimson forms work brilliantly in a sun-soaked, exotic garden, alongside large foliage and tropical flowers, such as *Canna*, *Dahlia*, and *Persicaria*.

It is a fantastic plant for coastal and windy sites (try a south-facing balcony), because it is tough and can take a battering. It thrives in very alkaline-rich, limey soils (all reasons why it's so often seen growing out of existing cracks in lime-based cement).

Invasiveness

Centranthus ruber's greatest attribute—and the very flaw that leads to its weedy classification—is its tendency to self-seed everywhere. Be ready. In Africa it is considered so invasive that it needs to be eradicated rather than grown.

Control

A garden full of *Centranthus ruber* alone would certainly be a pretty one (and one that you can easily achieve), but should you wish to allow other plants a look-in, cut off the flower heads as they turn to

reduce seed production. Remove any unwanted seedlings that sneak through. Growing the plant on a patio away from gravel and soil helps somewhat, especially if it's sheltered from wind. Larger shrubs and ground cover also help limit the area over which *Centranthus ruber* can grow, because they cover the soil.

Flower colors will mix over time if you let the plant self-seed, so remove the colors you don't want as soon as the flowers come up.

Cultivated varieties

Centranthus ruber "Albus" is the pure white cultivar and is available online and from nurseries.

Horsetail

Equisetum hyemale

This is an incredibly architectural plant with bolt-upright, spear-like stems in a contemporary black and green that can make a strong and modern statement. It is ideal for minimalist gardens and urban patios or balconies and as a focal point in a foliage garden.

Care: 1/5

Effort: 3/5

Rebelliousness: 4/5 (in water)

Plant family: Equisetaceae

Max size: 39½in (100cm) tall, 8in (20cm) wide

Color: green and black

Flowers: none

Pot friendly: yes

Soil: constantly damp

Situation: sun, part shade

Range: Europe, America (USDA hardiness zones 3–11), Australia, Asia, Russia

Origin: cool regions of the Northern Hemisphere

Historically *Equisetum hyemale* has been used (and in some places still is used) as a scourer—its UK common name is "scouring rush"—because broken pieces of dried stem are so rough and strong that they scrub away the caked-on bits on cooking utensils and dishes. Try it yourself.

Equisetum hyemale is deciduous: it dies back in winter, then shoots straight back in spring. It grows only in very damp soil, making it perfect for gardeners who overwater. Choose a pot that is very water retentive, such as those made from metal, fiberglass or glazed terracotta (normal terracotta dries compost out too quickly). Also consider blocking or partially blocking drainage holes to retain water and prevent the roots escaping the pot. Most plants would drown like this, but as a natural pond-marginal or bog plant *Equisetum hyemale* will thrive in this soggy situation. Never let it dry out.

Did you know?
Horsetails now have only one genus, "Equisetum," and are among the oldest-living fossils on Earth. Hundreds of millions of years ago they grew as trees up to 90 feet (30m) tall. Some of their closest relatives are the ferns. Neither plant family flowers, instead reproducing through spores.

Bringing *Equisetum hyemale* into your garden
If you know where the plants grow, and you're sure what you're getting, dig some up. However, it's best to buy this one online from a reputable supplier to ensure you bring the correct plant into your garden. The risk is that instead you find the extremely invasive, smaller garden weed *Equisetum arvense* (see p.27), which thrives in dry soils as well as damp—you've been warned!

For planting, *Equisetum hyemale* makes a great, low, transparent hedge. When you're seated it helps you feel enclosed, while still allowing you to peek through—a little like a very tough grass. It works very well in a long trough or row of pots for repetition, or as a striking feature in a single pot at the end of a path. The black joints up the stem suit black and gray pots, in particular.

Invasiveness
In suitable wetland areas, *Equisetum hyemale* can be invasive, particularly in parts of Australia. It spreads by vigorous underground rhizomes—new shoots grow upward along these. The plant produces spores and can also grow this way.

Control
If you grow *Equisetum hyemale* in a container in a garden away from ponds and rivers, it is unlikely it will spread at all.

Cultivated varieties
None known.

Orange hawkweed

Pilosella aurantiaca

The first time I stumbled upon the orange flowers of *Pilosella aurantiaca* it was alone among duller ornamentals and its flowers beamed out like glowing amber jewels. With its stylish combination of orange on black and squared petals it is the perfect plant for trendy urban gardens and industrial designs.

Care: 0/5

Effort: 3/5

Rebelliousness: 3/5

Plant family: Asteraceae

Max size: 12in (30cm) tall, 8in (20cm) wide

Color: rich orange

Flowers: June–September

Pot friendly: yes

Soil: any well drained

Situation: full sun, part shade

Range: global (USDA hardiness zones 5–10)

Origin: central and southern Europe

Originally from central and southern Europe, *Pilosella aurantiaca* is a tough cookie, growing boldly like its relatives *Taraxacum officinale* and *Hypochaeris radicata*. *Pilosella aurantiaca* benefits from having an inconspicuous, low-growing rosette of simple green leaves. Its long stems produce flowers all summer, holding them high above the foliage. The flower stem and unopened buds are almost black, contrasting sharply with the deep-orange petals that are cut like dandelions with squared ends.

Pots are the perfect home for *Pilosella aurantiaca* because it is a drought-tolerant plant, preferring light soils that are free-draining in full to partial sun. Naturally, it grows in thin, nutrient-poor soil in waste areas or in low-growing grass—it looks particularly good dotted through lawns.

Did you know?
The plant's UK common name, fox and cubs, refers to a family of foxes snuggled together, the open flower the parent, the buds its cubs.

Bringing *Pilosella aurantiaca* into your garden
As the flowers mature you'll notice fluffy, gray seed heads appearing. Gather these seeds when they fall easily, then sprinkle them into a pot. Alternatively, dig up a plant and transfer it to your container. *Pilosella aurantiaca* is also available online as seeds and small inexpensive plug plants.

Position a pot full in front of concrete walls, lush green foliage, or metal to further contrast those orange flowers. The effect looks great in tropical and exotic gardens.

Invasiveness
The plant spreads by creeping runners that start new plants a short distance from the parent. If the plant is growing in lawns (where it looks quite exotic) or garden beds, this spread can be fairly rapid. It's a plant that successfully reproduces by seeds carried on the wind, too.

Control
Growing in pots completely contains the vegetative runner spread. To control the seed spread, you have to deadhead the flowers as they finish and before the plant produces seed. Keep a close eye—the change is rapid. If the plants are growing in your garden, invest some time and a bit of muscle power and you will easily dig them out.

Cultivated varieties
None known.

Chapter 7

Weeds for Ground Cover

Fight weeds with weeds. Plants that form a tight mat over the soil suppress the germination of other plants—and that means that with ground cover, you can control what pops up in your beds. In design terms, ground cover serves many purposes. It gives a sense of space above—offering gaps and breathing room among busy plantings, just as we expect from a lawn. It can add bold waves of color, or tidy up a garden bed, or bring beauty in problem areas where nothing else will grow. In the world of ground covers, weeds are your allies.

Scarlet pimpernel

Anagallis arvensis

I first spotted *Anagallis arvensis* on my community garden in my prairie-flower garden bed. Its small, orange flowers were noticeably different to other weeds and wildflowers, making a welcome addition among tall, brown grasses.

Care: 1/5

Effort: 2/5

Rebelliousness: 1/5

Plant family: Primulaceae

Max size: 4in (10cm) tall, limitless spread

Color: dusky orange or occasionally blue

Flowers: all summer

Pot friendly: yes

Soil: prefers dry, nutrient-poor, sandy soil, but can grow anywhere

Situation: sun to part shade

Range: global (USDA hardiness zones 6–11)

Origin: Mediterranean region

Anagallis arvensis is a very low-growing plant with a sprawling habit but few leaves, which means other plants can grow through it. It's a very courteous weed: it scrambles around a garden causing no harm to other plants whatsoever. Its upward-facing flowers are small but packed with color—on a sunny day these tiny spots of dusty orange open wide and spread thinly across the weed, like stars in the night sky.

In dull weather the flowers close, giving the plant one of its common names, shepherd's weatherglass, although you'd hope a shepherd wouldn't need a flower to indicate whether or not it's raining. Scarlet pimpernel, the more widely used common name, is famously known as the title of the play and book by Baroness Orczy. The protagonist leads a double life, saving people under a secret identity, known only by his emblem, the flower of *Anagallis arvensis*.

Bringing *Anagallis arvensis* into your garden

This plant doesn't like being moved—plus it grows quickly—so it's best to grow it from seed. It flowers and seeds freely all summer, forming little round seed capsules. Keep an eye on these and as soon as some turn brown, give them a little shake and listen for the quiet rustle. If you hear it, break the capsule to extract the seeds. Scatter these in your garden where you'd like the plant to grow.

Because it doesn't form a dense ground cover, *Anagallis arvensis* works really well as very low ground cover, adding some unobtrusive color between other, bigger, bolder plants. On my community garden I grow it between various types of ornamental grass and tall perennials, including *Sorghastrum nutans*, *Deschampsia cespitosa*, and *Astrantia major* subsp. *involucrata* "Shaggy." It looks particularly exquisite flowering between *Armeria* "Ballerina Red," *Kniphofia* "Tawny King," and the brown grass, *Carex buchananii*.

Work with *Anagallis arvensis* so that it becomes a background color to your planty painting.

Invasiveness

The seeds remain viable for some time, but *Anagallis arvensis* isn't really an invasive plant. It rarely grows in such numbers as to be a problem and tougher plants can crowd it out.

Control

Once it starts seeding, it's hard to prevent *Anagallis arvensis* coming back, as the seeds will lay dormant in the soil. However, as an arable weed, it thrives best in disturbed and bare soil, such as soil you're digging or when you're planting other plants. If you pull out the plant (which is quite easy to do), take care not to disturb the soil too much and it will eventually stop coming back.

Cultivated varieties

None. However, there is a naturally occurring sapphire-blue-flowered variety. This is quite rare in the UK (but oddly far more common than the orange flower across Europe), so I wouldn't advise collecting it unless you're lucky enough to happen upon a particularly large colony. In that case taking three or four seeds will be fine.

Lesser celandine

Ficaria verna

A swathe of bright yellow *Ficaria verna* in spring is a cheering sight that will brighten any tricky corner of a garden. Use it en masse to create a sudden and bold blanket of yellow in those early spring months—nothing will better proclaim that winter is over.

Care: 0/5

Effort: 3/5

Rebelliousness: 3/5

Plant family:	Ranunculaceae
Max size:	2in (5cm) tall, limitless spread
Color:	yellow
Flowers:	February–April
Pot friendly:	yes
Soil:	any damp
Situation:	shade or part sun
Range:	global (USDA hardiness zones 4–8)
Origin:	Europe, western Asia

Owing to *Ficaria verna*'s want to take over, try to avoid introducing it in herbaceous gardens. However, it works well in a shrubbery, below hedges, on slopes, and in woodland settings (areas where you want to stop other weeds taking over). Meadows are another good setting, where the hurly-burly of other plants keeps *Ficaria verna* in check.

Did you know?
William Wordsworth wrote three poems about *Ficaria verna*, his favorite weedy flower. It even receives a little mention in C.S. Lewis's *The Lion, the Witch and the Wardrobe*.

Bringing *Ficaria verna* into your garden
Introducing the plant is very easy: simply dig up a piece with a good chunk of root and then plant it. Grow it in tough corners where other plants won't grow, particularly in dry shade beneath deciduous trees, hedges, or shrubs, when bare in spring, allow the plant sunlight and rain while it's growing. *Ficaria verna* will then go dormant for the rest of the year as the canopy closes over it. Such a thoughtful palette of succession planting will create color year-round, and at the same time suppress the growth of other weeds that could smother the valuable woody plants. Larger shrubs and trees won't be bothered by the thick layer of *Ficaria verna*, as their roots will grow beneath the smaller plant.

Invasiveness
Ficaria verna doesn't seed around much, but where it's happy it will spread quite quickly, overtaking other small, less-robust plants plants; it can be invasive on the east coast and some of the Midwest and Pacific Northwest. For example, *Ficaria verna* can eventually crowd out primulas and will cause problems in herbaceous gardens where it's hard to weed out. It has tough root tubers that store energy and multiply, while above-ground bulbils form on the stems. These root, creating new plants. It's this ability to store energy and root living plants (the bulbils) that makes *Ficaria verna* so successful in problem areas of the garden.

Control
The best control is containment. Don't grow *Ficaria verna* in a garden with other plants that are less vigorous. Instead, keep it to dry-shade corners and growing among bigger, tougher plants (see above).

If you do have it in an unwanted place, unfortunately the only real means of control is digging out over a few seasons, or a glyphosate-based weed killer. In a garden bed, really this means you'll need to remove all other plants before you spray, and then spray the *Ficaria verna* a number of times until it is gone.

Cultivated varieties
There are lots of cultivars, many with black-marked, blotchy leaves. "Brazen Hussy" has very dark, almost black leaves that add extra

contrast to the flowers; while "Flore Pleno" has double, water-lily-like flowers with green centers.

English ivy

Hedera helix

As a climber *Hedera helix* is a much-feared, hard-to-control, romping beast. There is, however, no denying its dark green beauty, often with white, marbled leaf veins. You can use it to cover completely the ground between trees and shrubs, and even in more contemporary settings in street plantings and next to patios.

Care: 0/5

Effort: 3/5

Rebelliousness: 3/5

☠

Plant family: Araliaceae

Max size: 8in (20cm) tall if prevented from climbing, limitless spread

Color: dark green

Flowers: n/a

Pot friendly: yes

Soil: any

Situation: sun to shade

Range: global (USDA hardiness zones 4–9)

Origin: Europe, western Asia

In its native Europe, *Hedera helix* is crucial for wildlife, providing shelter, food, and nectar for pollinating insects, especially in winter.

Its greatest characteristic, however, is its ability to grow where little else can, even in the deepest, driest shade. If you maintain it well, it will create a fantastic, dark understory to brighter shrubs, pots, or statues. Carefully placed bright flowers will glow against *Hedera helix*.

This climber will grow across the ground until it finds something to climb up—if you plant it in the middle of bare soil, it will spread outward to completely cover the area. As a tough plant it can handle some trampling and as much cutting back as you care to give it. When *Hedera helix* is on the ground, use a lawnmower on a high setting to mow the plant occasionally, avoiding the very woody parts, which will damage the mower. Afterward it'll look a bit messy, but soon after fresh, bright green leaves will emerge. You can also clip it with sheers to maintain straight edges—say, along a path. Its resilience and scope for shaping means *Hedera helix* provides limitless possibility as a 2D form of ground-cover topiary.

Did you know?
The leaves of *Hedera helix* have been celebrated in thousands of artworks, including in Vincent van Gogh's painting *Tree Trunks with Ivy*, where *Hedera helix* is shown both as a climber and ground cover. The plant's pattern has adorned fashionable dresses and buildings, including (famously) Victorian textile designer William Morris's wallpapers and fabrics.

Bringing *Hedera helix* into your garden
It's best to introduce ivy as a rooted plant, which you can buy in any garden center, or else dig one up. It's easy to grow from root cuttings, too. Yank a good-size piece off a plant, plonk it in some damp soil and the plant should root in a few weeks.

Try growing the plant beneath shrubs that you cut back each year, such as *Euphorbia characias* subsp. *wulfenii*, *Sambucus nigra* f. *porphyrophylla* "Black Lace," *Buddleja davidii* (see p.158), and *Hydrangea*. The cutting back prevents *Hedera helix* from growing vertically up the stems. Tall *Narcissus pseudonarcissus* and *Hyacinthoides non-scripta* (see p.22), grown from strong bulbs planted through *Hedera helix*, works really well.

Invasiveness
Leave your *Hedera helix* unchecked for a few years and it will become invasive (it's considered a noxious weed in Oregon and Washington, and invasive in several other states). As it spreads it will root, forming tough, woody stems. It's at its most invasive when given the chance to climb up trees, walls or fences, where it will rocket skyward. On

the ground it's slower growing—especially in dry soils—but will root itself fairly deeply, making it quite difficult to pull out.

Control
Unlike weeds that seed themselves freely, ivy is easier to control. Although it does seed around, it produces relatively few seedlings. Planting in deep, dry shade will slow the plant's spread, as will regular mowing or cutting back (see above). Cutting back older, thick stems at the base of the plant and removing them will reduce vigor. Watch out for stems that climb up nearby trees or structures: cut them off at the base and pull them off once dead.

The main control to worry about is a mature plant's rate of spread. You'll need to cut thick, woody stems with shears, but they are quite brittle and will easily snap. It's easy to leave segments of root in the soil, which means a new plant will grow back—plan for a second round of weeding to catch these rebels.

Cultivated varieties
There are hundreds of different cultivated varieties of *Hedera helix*, including variegated "Glacier," and the unusual leaf forms of "Pedata" and "Maple Leaf."

Purple wood sorrel

Oxalis corniculata var. atropurpurea

One of the most annoying weeds in gardeners' most-hated lists (if your garden has it, you'll know it), *Oxalis corniculata* var. *atropurpurea* is nonetheless a quite distinct and refined plant.

Care: 1/5

Effort: 5/5

Rebelliousness: 5/5

Plant family: Oxalidaceae

Max size: 4in (10cm) tall, limitless spread

Color: purple-brown leaves, yellow flowers

Flowers: May–September

Pot friendly: yes

Soil: any

Situation: full sun

Range: global (USDA zones unknown)

Origin: Europe, Asia

There is debate over this weed's exact origin. Some say Mexico, others say the Mediterranean—although we do know that it was introduced to North America in the 1700s. Perhaps no one wants to take the blame.

Oxalis corniculata var. *atropurpurea* pops up everywhere—lawns, bare soil, pots, cracks in paving … everywhere. If you can look past the messy, unplanned arrival in such places, you'll find a delicately colored, low-growing, tough plant. During their growth, the neatly edged leaves give a beautiful range of colors: dusty dark green, then tints of purple that turn a dull, purple-brown. Throughout the whole summer, small, rich sulfur-yellow flowers appear in sharp contrast. In summer it is very effective ground cover, but the plant is deciduous, dying back in winter and reducing its ability to prevent the growth of other weeds in the colder months. I love the look of it so much that Philippa Borough, the owner of Ulting Wick garden in Essex, UK, has nicknamed the plants "Jacks."

Bringing *Oxalis corniculata* var. *atropurpurea* into your garden
You can grow this plant easily from seeds, but catching the seeds is tricky! *Oxalis corniculata* var. *atropurpurea* quickly forms upright fruit capsules, which entertainingly explode on contact (try capturing that explosion in slow motion on your smartphone). Puff open a brown paper bag and position it near the seed capsule, touch the capsule and then attempt to gather as many seeds into the bag as you can. Sprinkle them where you want the plant to grow.

Once you've established *Oxalis corniculata* var. *atropurpurea*, consider it a core element of your designs. Its coloring naturally lends itself to a contemporary combination with gray- and terracotta-colored paving and pots. Grown along paths or with soft-colored *Geum* "Totally Tangerine" or "Mai Tai," it acts as a beautiful carpet backdrop. *Oxalis corniculata* var. *atropurpurea* is also a perfect companion to grass garden beds and prairies, where the larger grasses easily outcompete it. The combination works particularly well with deciduous grasses, such as *Calamagrostis* x *acutiflora* in fall. It's a perfect match for hot and tropical garden beds, working with yellows, reds, and oranges, and an excellent understory to *Ulex europaeus* (see p.166) and *Berberis*. When you see it alone in a terracotta pot, it's hard to imagine this is a weed.

Invasiveness
Oxalis corniculata var. *atropurpurea* spreads mainly via the explosive seeds, which are catapulted up to 6 feet (2m) away from the parent. It is a highly invasive mini plant in a world of more powerful giants. A thick mat of shallow roots matches its small size. If you don't already have it, do think carefully before introducing it, because once established you'll have it for ever. That said, although it can smother the germinating seeds of other plants, it won't affect more established plants at all as they simply shade and crowd it out. If you do want to grow other plants from seed, simply clear the area of *Oxalis corniculata* var. *atropurpurea* and other weeds, until those plants are well grown.

Control
The roots are tricky to hoe, making it difficult to weed out established plants, but you'll easily lift out young ones. In small gardens it's very easy to keep *Oxalis corniculata* var. *atropurpurea* under control—but in larger gardens you'll have something of a battle, making it better to use any existing plants in your garden palette, working with them rather than against them. Using weed killer is pointless, because a new plant will grow from seeds in the soil.

Cultivated varieties
None known.

Sweet violet

Viola odorata

Few sights are as showstopping as the thick ground cover of *Viola odorata* in spring. This is a fast-growing plant that creates dense mats of shiny, green leaves and a spectacular display of violet, blue, or white. It has a sweet scent.

Care: 0/5

Effort: 2/5

Rebelliousness: 3/5

Plant family: Violaceae

Max size: 4in (10cm) tall, limitless spread

Color: dark purple, white, light blue

Flowers: March–May

Pot friendly: yes

Soil: any moist but well drained

Situation: part shade

Range: Europe, America (USDA hardiness zones 4–9), Australasia, Asia

Origin: Europe, Asia

Grown en masse, *Viola odorata* is to purple what daffodils are to yellow—the flowers create a single block of eye-catching color; the bigger the block, the greater the impact. Grow *Viola odorata* at the front of garden beds, along path edges, and into lawns (it can handle the occasional trampling). Even consider using it to replace the entire lawn if the lawn is more for show than for use.

Sheets of purple *Viola odorata* are particularly surprising because the color appears without warning. Most other spring plants grow long leaves as a precursor to flower, but *Viola odorata*'s flowers open quickly above low leaves, catching us off guard and adding to the delight. The little, shiny leaves create an inconspicuous, tidy mat of greenery for most of the year when the plant is not in flower and make a good backdrop to other plants.

Did you know?
The scented flowers of *Viola odorata* are edible. They're slightly sweet, so you can use them to garnish salads or desserts. You can also make a syrup with them—apparently it is good for coughs, but equally it tastes good in cocktails, diluted as a cordial, and over ice cream.

Bringing *Viola odorata* into your garden
Transplant a little rooted piece of the plant at any time; or collect seeds when the seed pods have turned brown and have started opening. The pods open into three segments, each lined with tiny brown seeds. Sprinkle the seeds where you want them to grow and mark the spot with a label.

The roots of *Viola odorata* are quite shallow and the plant prefers growing in part shade on the edges of damp garden beds, replicating its natural habitat of woodland edges and hedges. Its ability to grow among taller plants means you can happily plant it in busy gardens and its shallow roots won't affect the growth of larger perennials or shrubs.

Shade from other plants won't affect *Viola odorata* all that much either. Try growing late-winter bulbs, such as *Galanthus*, *Iris reticulata* or *Crocus tommasinianus* through *Viola odorata*. Position them all at the base of a herbaceous perennial or deciduous shrub, such as *Buddleja davidii* (see p.158), *Philadelphus*, or *Hydrangea*. The bulbs will flower before *Viola odorata* takes over, then the shrubs happily succeed them later in summer.

Invasiveness
Viola ordorata is slightly invasive, because once a little clump is established, it will very quickly spread by rhizomes and cast seeds around the garden. You'll spot it cropping up all over the place: in gravel, along wall edges, and so on. However, its spread rarely poses a problem for other plants.

Control
In garden beds it provides very little competition and larger plants will quickly crowd it out. Around the rest of the garden, however, dig out by hand or hoe new seedlings as you see them.

Cultivated varieties
There are many cultivars, as well as naturally occurring white and pale blue varieties. "Königin Charlotte" (Queen Charlotte), which was introduced at the start of the twentieth century in Germany, has upward-facing flowers; "Reign de Neiges" has almost white flowers.

Claudia West — Principal, Phyto Studio

Landscape architect and plantswoman on the East Coast of the USA, renowned for low-maintenance, plant-community-based design. Co-author of the seminal book, *Planting in a Post-Wild World*.

We hear a lot about plant communities, but what actually are they? People know very little about plant communities, we're just starting to understand. They're social networks, densely layered, incredibly diverse and sophisticated in their interactions. They have evolved over hundreds of thousands of years in some places. Plants collaborate, compete, and communicate with one another. Not through the language we know, but an incredibly sophisticated chemical language.

What are the benefits of a plant-community approach to design? Traditional planting selects species for aesthetic reasons: pretty flowers, pollinators. Take a closer look and you see bare soil or mulch underneath these eye-candy plants. This is where weeds grow, this is where maintenance cost comes from, this is where water runs off and you're just not using that space efficiently. By using a plant-community-based approach many of these gaps can be filled with plants that, for example, cover ground to reduce weed pressure and bring down maintenance cost, soaking up more stormwater, while cooling and cleaning air more effectively.

Can they be beautiful, too? Designed plant communities have this spirit of the wild, they're dynamic and remind us of something we've lost, but something we remember because we evolved in it. There's a deep emotional connection between a plant community and something that intuitively feels right and inspiring because it builds a bridge to our past, to our evolution in nature. They're still artful, following core rules of design, but this spirit is refreshing. You can see New Yorkers smile when they're up on the Highline, it's obvious and powerful. There's also a beauty—which is more important to millennial gardeners than to anybody—designing not just for people, but seeing insects and birds thriving, making a landscape come to life. It matters more and more to the younger generation to do the right thing.

You mentioned you have an interest in weeds, where does that stem from? I have deep respect for weeds. I wish half our horticultural plants would have the resilience and survival tactics that weeds have. I find it frustrating that plants the nursery industry spends millions breeding start dying as soon as you put them in the ground; they're not built for this world. Most landscapes don't have the luxury of a maintained garden, it's sink or swim. I'm trying to fold what we call weeds into our plant palettes because we need plants to survive without human help. I want my plantings to survive me, quite frankly. We need things that behave like weeds, that will still be there ten to twenty years from today. I'm even conflicted about using the word weed—it really depends on the project site.

Which US weeds are the most frustrating for gardeners? There is a different category of weeds, those of exotic origin and new to this country that have no or very few connections with wildlife here. They destroy ecosystems, invade gardens, and create a real nightmare because they don't pair with other plants, making monocultures. Things like *Microstegium vimineum* (see p.29). It invaded this part of the US about ten years ago, and is a weed I could not live with in my garden. It's allelopathic, which means it wages chemical warfare with other plants, stopping seed germination and growth. Things like that or mile-a-minute vine and *Kudzu* (see p.32), they're no-gos.

Which weeds have you used in designs? *Achillea millefolium*, various species of violets, *Daucus carota* (see p.54). Things like *Erigeron annuus* and milkweeds, like common milkweed, *Asclepias syriaca*, are valuable assets to more naturalistic plant communities. It's fine to leave them.

Is there one weed that's a favorite of yours? I'm adding violets for weed suppression, ground cover and because, according to entomologists, they feed at least twenty-nine *Lepidoptera* species (moths and butterflies). I'm designing the friendship garden for the US National Arboretum in Washington, D.C. The team almost fainted when they saw my plant list because it included violets, which they'd been weeding out for decades!

I'm really interested in the weeds we see popping up around cities and human-made habitats… Urban weeds are probably the things that will save the world— they're so important. Using wild, spontaneous plants that pop up everywhere is the most sustainable way of making cities greener. If I'm excited about anything, it's that.

Chapter 8

Weeds for Steps and Walls

I always think that in a city, with a landscape of brick and concrete, it's satisfying when nature pushes back, popping through cracks with tiny pockets of color. Walls and steps can be beautiful garden features; they also offer a chance to grow unique weeds. Chosen carefully, some weeds bring color and softness to these hard, angular surfaces, enhancing and framing the building materials. Growing in tiny cracks and gaps, these plant daredevils won't compromise the structure of their habitat, and they require no care whatsoever—perfect! Better yet, you don't even need a garden, just a wall.

Bellflower

Campanula poscharskyana
and *Campanula portenschlagiana*

Bellflowers are one of summer's most delicate sights. Different species grow in meadows, on cliffs, in gardens, and now—thanks to two garden escapees— on walls and steps in urban spaces. Don't be fooled by their apparent delicateness, these plants are as hard as nails.

Care: 1/5

Effort: 2/5

Rebelliousness: 3/5

Plant family: Campanulaceae

Max size: 8in (20cm) tall, unlimited spread

Color: light blue to purple

Flowers: May–October

Pot friendly: yes

Soil: any very well drained

Situation: part sun, shade

Range: Europe, Australasia, Japan, North America (USDA hardiness zones 3–8)

Origin: central and southern Europe (specifically Croatia, Bosnia, and Herzegovina)

Campanula poscharskyana and *Campanula portenschlagiana* are alpines from the central and southern regions of Europe. They love growing in severe drainage and full sun on rock screes and cliffs—which explains why they want to grow in a sharply draining substrate with little nutrient, and why they were first introduced as rock-garden plants. As with many wall-lovers, these plants enjoy alkaline conditions, which are provided by the lime in the cement of mortar.

Campanula poscharskyana and *Campanula portenschlagiana* are very similar in appearance but once you spot the differences, you'll always see them. *Campanula poscharskyana*, the trailing bellflower, is slightly looser in habit than *Campanula portenschlagiana* and always has pale, sky-blue flowers; its petal lobes are longer. *Campanula portenschlagiana*, the wall bellflower, is tighter with pale blue to violet–purple flowers and shorter petal lobes. Both plants enjoy growing in full sun and develop a mass of tiny fibrous roots that lock them into the mortar between bricks and gaps in the paving of steps. *Campanula portenschlagiana* is slightly more drought-tolerant, meaning it can grow higher on walls in tougher conditions.

Traditional brick walls and stone-slab steps provide the ideal environments for these plants to self-seed gently into the smallest of cracks in the mortar, their fine roots using existing spaces without causing damage. The plants flower from spring all the way through to late fall.

Although there are modern uses for these plants (particularly if you find a vivid violet-purple variety of *Campanula portenschlagiana*), they suit traditional and cottage gardens. Weathered brick, natural gray stone, and dry-stone walls provide backdrops that combine well with the pastel of the flower. In a raised bed you can allow the plants to propagate at the foot of the bed's retaining wall, below the main planting, as if the flowers are spilling over.

Bringing *Campanula* into your garden

In spring, find a large clump, making sure the flowers are the color you want. Dig out a piece being very careful not to rip the tiny fibrous roots. These plants have a tendency to wilt almost immediately with too much damage, even when they previously appeared perfectly happy.

Push the roots of your new plant into a regular gap in your own wall. Do this during wet weather to help the plant establish in its new home. (Plants growing in walls are hard to water yourself.) Alternatively, if it's easier, plant into soil or a gap at the foot of a wall or step and let the plant climb upwards gradually over a year or two. Another option is to start at the top—allowing the plant gently to seed and spread downward in the future.

Otherwise, you can collect seeds or buy them online. Try a combination of placing the seeds themselves into cracks outside in spring, and into plugs inside, which you can then transplant, just as you would if you'd dug out a plant you'd found growing wild.

Use one of these plants to soften the corner of a step, or to grow along the top of a low wall or even in paving cracks at the foot of walls. They add a subliminal frame grown in diagonally opposite corners, highlighting the beauty of the stonework. Although they can spread to cover large areas, they look best if restricted to smaller spots.

Invasiveness

Neither *Campanula* is particularly invasive, although both will spread and can smother other, very small plants. Once established, both will pop up in various places, but never grow so high as to be out of reach. Nor will they take over.

Control

Owing to their fibrous roots, these *Campanula* are extremely easy to rip out. They might grow back occasionally, but just pull them out again.

Cultivated varieties

There are many cultivated varieties of both these plants. Look out for different colors and shapes each year, usually produced and sold in nurseries as alpine, container, or bedding plants. *Campanula portenschlagiana* "White Get Mee" has pure white flowers, as does *Campanula poscharskyana* under various different cultivar names, including "E.H. Frost" and "Hirsch White."

Ivy-leaved toadflax

Cymbalaria muralis

Sometimes weeds can look delicate, but it's a trick! Weeds always have a means for rapid growth and reproduction—even the pretty, lilac, romantic-looking *Cymbalaria muralis*. This plant can grow in a mind-bogglingly sparse amount of growing media, happily populating walls, even during drought.

Care: 0/5

Effort: 3/5

Rebelliousness: 3/5

Plant family: Plantaginaceae

Max size: 4in (10cm) tall, unlimited spread

Color: lilac

Flowers: April–October

Pot friendly: yes

Soil: any very well drained

Situation: shade, part shade

Range: global (USDA hardiness zones 5–8)

Origin: southern Europe

Cymbalaria muralis is reminiscent of the floral patterns that adorn the edges of Roman tapestries. Wire-thin red stems are spread with sparse, small leaves said to resemble *Hedera helix* (see p.132), explaining the UK's common name for the plant: ivy-leaved toadflax. Even if the resemblance isn't clear, the leaves are very pretty, with lovely cloud-like curves—they look shiny and vibrant all year round. The plant's stems will root where they touch a suitable substrate.

Flowering for most of the year with tiny lilac-and-white flowers, this plant always looks good. Best-suited to traditional gardens, it will nonetheless also work in modern spaces that have a cool, calm color palette. Originating from the sun-bleached Mediterranean, it can be combined with any plant from that region, as well as with plants that have soft, gray foliage and light, smaller flowers.

One of *Cymbalaria muralis's* greatest assets is the fact it acts as a tiny, self-clinging climber. Imagine this little flower twining up the legs of a table, anchoring it visually to a garden. Climbing seemingly impossible faces is what *Cymbalaria muralis* does best, with an enviably relaxed, soft, free-flowing style, and purple-lilac color.

Bringing *Cymbalaria muralis* into your garden

Bide your time and *Cymbalaria muralis* will eventually appear. If you really do happen to have the only garden in the world without it, you can dig up a little clump and replant it during a rainy week in spring, ensuring it's watered; or try to collect the seeds. You'll find the seeds at the end of the flowering stem, tucked away. Release the seeds, store them in a paper bag and then sow them exactly where you want the plant to grow. In a wall, try stuffing a little compost into a crack— you won't need much—add the seeds, water them without washing out the compost and wait for the magic to happen.

It blends beautifully with whites and other pastel-colored flowers. Growing *Cymbalaria muralis* on a wall behind or under (say, on the wall of a raised bed) lavenders, rosemary and roses works well—it prefers a little dappled shade. For a more contemporary pairing, grow *Cymbalaria muralis* in a garden with perennials that you might see in modern, urban designs: *Gaura*, *Salvia*, *Echinacea*, and *Verbena*. Ideally, choose plants that "mingle" well with others, where flowers and foliage are happy to weave into each other.

In terms of landscaping, *Cymbalaria muralis* suits gray best: choose steps of gray stone or limestone, dry-stone walls, and even cement. (The crispness of cement highlights the plant's form.) It's most at home in dry-stone walls, where it can grip and spread as easily as other plants do in garden beds. Like most wall-dwellers, little clumps enhance the rest of the wall, rather than detract. Allow it to form sizeable clumps for the small flowers to have impact en masse.

Invasiveness

Having had *Cymbalaria muralis* in my garden and having left it, it's really quite amazing how quickly it grows when your back is turned. Speed of growth and spread is a strong asset for creating impact in one growing season, but rooting into crevices and self-seeding mean it can quickly take over small areas. When pulled out it can regrow from roots left behind.

There's no need to worry about a garden takeover, though: *Cymbalaria muralis* can't compete well with other plants, which is why it prefers to climb walls away from them.

Control

Pull out the plant by hand but make sure you get all of the roots otherwise it will regenerate. To eradicate the plant entirely, you'll have to repeat this process regularly for a couple of seasons. However, if your wall is a good spot for *Cymbalaria muralis*, the likelihood of it reseeding naturally from another source is high, usually thanks to birds. Be vigilant!

Cultivated varieties

Cymbalaria muralis "Alba" has pure white flowers that make for a great plant, but never quite look as good as the species that has lilac flowers.

Rock fumewort

Pseudofumaria lutea

If there is one plant that embodies the modern age it's *Pseudofumaria lutea*. A flower of our time, it makes a home for itself on walls of every city and town with fairly cool, humid climates in summer. Its masses of small, glowing, yellow flowers challenge traditional gardening values; and its shape—on close inspection—is quite futuristic.

Care: 0/5

Effort: 2/5

Rebelliousness: 4/5

Plant family: Papaveraceae

Max size: 12in (30cm) tall, 12in (30cm) wide

Color: yellow

Flowers: April–October

Pot friendly: yes

Soil: any very well drained

Situation: part shade

Range: global (USDA zones unknown)

Origin: Switzerland, Italy

Grown centuries ago as an ornamental, *Pseudofumaria lutea* sits in the same plant family as all poppies and is a short-lived perennial, living for a number of years until the next generation takes over from the parent plant's seeds. It originates from the southern Alps and can withstand temperatures as low as -30°F (-35°C).

Not easily found in the US, you're most likely to discover it growing in cracks on the sides, tops, and bases of walls in sunny positions with some shade. If you stop to look at it, it's a beautifully formed plant. Its leaves are finely divided, almost fern-like, creating a soft tussock of pale, green leaves that always look good. The small trumpet-shaped flowers are like tiny spaceships. They are strong yellow at the tip fading to a pale, almost translucent yellow at the back with a touch of fresh green.

Bringing *Pseudofumaria lutea* into your garden

Pseudofumaria lutea is best introduced as seeds, which are available online or which you can collect easily from the plants' tiny seed pods. Once dry, the pods will open and then seeds will drop out for you to collect in a paper bag. Drop the seeds into cracks and crevices, water and wait.

Try growing some other yellow flowers, such as *Meconopsis cambrica* (see p.100) or *Primula vulgaris* (see p.23), in a bed or pot at the foot of the wall where *Pseudofumaria lutea* is growing—this will add to the sense of your planting being intentional. Equally, light yellows work wonderfully with dark greens, making evergreen hedges and shrubs, such as *Taxus baccata* and *Laurus nobilis* cultivars, good companions. For a tropical and urban look, consider plants such as *Fatsia japonica* and *Fatsia polycarpa*, large ferns, tree ferns, or *Mahonia*.

In a suitable wall it will make its home in little clumps, which, owing to the yellow, creates a bold, good-looking focal point, especially on darker brick. Like all wall-dwelling plants, *Pseudofumaria lutea* never quite fills the whole vertical area. If you have too many of these plants, they can look scruffy, so limit them to a few spots, repeated, to give some order. *Pseudofumaria lutea* looks fantastic on top of a wall in a large clump, perhaps repeated in the diagonally opposite lower corner.

On the wall itself *Pseudofumaria lutea* is interesting alongside wall-loving ferns such as *Asplenium scolopendrium* (see p.116) for contrasting foliage and *Polypodium vulgare*, creating a slightly tropical look.

Pseudofumaria lutea shows its full design potential in urban settings placed against copper, a contrasting navy blue background, or a complementary dark color. Painting walls or growing the weed next to doors, pots, or furniture of these colors really sets it off. As

Pseudofumaria lutea consists of many tiny leaves and flowers, it works well as a backdrop to larger objects with clean lines that cut across its collage of shapes. Objects such as pots and the edge of a step are perfect. Plants with large leaves work well, too.

Invasiveness

This isn't a very invasive plant. It will reseed readily—but not excessively—popping up in different places. It rarely outcompetes other plants.

Control

You'll easily identify this weed by its leaf shape. When you do, pull it out by hand—you'll have to keep doing this as other seeds germinate.

Cultivated varieties

None known.

Fern

Various species

Ferns bring lush, green foliage to shady garden situations with many plants having evolved to thrive on vertical rock faces. Although you might be forgiven for thinking that all ferns look the same, even wall-dwelling ferns have noticeably different frond shapes. The following are the best ferns for temperate climates with good rainfall.

Care: 1/5

Effort: 1/5

Rebelliousness: 2/5

Plant division: Polypodiophyta

Max size: 12in (30cm) tall, 12in (30cm) wide

Color: green

Flowers: n/a

Pot friendly: yes

Soil: any very well drained

Situation: shade (although will handle some sun)

Range: global (USDA zones unknown)

Origin: global

Most of the wall-dwelling ferns we know love alkaline conditions, making the cement mortar (which is based on lime) the perfect habitat for them. They bring luxurious green to even the dullest, harshest corners of brick and concrete—breathing life into the seemingly most inhospitable environments, and adding a softness and vitality.

Asplenium trichomanes is a tiny fern that forms 6–8in-wide (15–20cm), starfish-shaped clumps with miniature divided fronds with black stems. It's a beautiful little plant that looks great in a gray, dry-stone wall, which will highlight the plant's shape, dark green leaves, and black stems. The much larger *Asplenium scolopendrium* (see p.116) also thrives in walls with its unique, tropical-esque fronds.

Polypodium vulgare (with chunky, tropical fronds) and *Polypodium cambricum* (with more traditional, divided fronds) are two ferns that form creeping rhizomes from which new fronds emerge at intervals. Owing to this habit of creeping around cracks and gaps, both these plants will slowly form clumps wherever they can get a foothold. Unlike many ferns that emerge in spring, *Polypodium* usually goes dormant in the heat of the summer when the old fronds crisp up and fall off (once they die, if they don't fall, they are best cut off). From mid-summer onward, new fronds will emerge, looking bright and fresh just as everything else in the garden is hitting its summer stride, adding a new point of interest. If the plants receive enough moisture, clumps of *Polypodium* on walls and steps can look luxurious and tropical. In areas of high rainfall or moisture, such as near the coast, they even grow in trees.

Did you know?
Ferns are living fossils, among the oldest species on Earth. They reproduce in quite an amazing way and they start life as an almost entirely different plant. When a fern spore germinates, it grows into a gametophyte, a tiny thumbnail-size disk of green that can look like lichen or moss. It's this plant that contains the eggs and sperm for reproduction, with fern sperm swimming through water to reach the eggs on other gametophytes. Only when the sperm fertilizes an egg can a new fern form, growing into another plant that is the larger, spore-producing stage (called the sporophyte) we recognize as a fern.

Bringing ferns into your garden
The best option is to buy plants from garden centers, or to find them growing out and about and transplant them. Give the plants a good soak for an hour or so, then poke their roots into a gap, making sure the roots are secure, but being very careful not to damage them too much. If conditions are right, the plants will continue growing and, over the years, will multiply and spread around. As with all wall planting, do this during damp weather—in spring or fall.

Grow ferns in the corners of steps or, for the smaller *Asplenium trichomanes*, along the vertical riser, being careful not to create a trip hazard. In urban situations encourage fern clumps in the harshest of shady spots down alleyways, in corners, and on the tops of walls—they will add green to otherwise depressing spaces. Cut off dead fronds to keep the plants looking their best.

Invasiveness
Ferns are not really invasive unless the conditions are absolutely perfect with lots of humid moisture, and rainfall. In St Ives, a seaside town in the UK, I've seen drainpipes and roofs entirely covered in carpets of fern.

Control
Pull out unwanted plants by hand when they are large enough to do so.

Cultivated varieties
Polypodium cambricum "Pulcherrimum Addison" has highly divided, shapely fronds that look architectural. The plant has a beautiful, light green color, keeping it fresh. *Polypodium vulgare* "Bifidomultifidum" has fronds that divide a random number of times, as well as slightly crested tips that form a fishtail shape, rather than a point, at the ends.

Moss

Various species

In the West, moss is so often seen as the enemy. Yet, in Japan, moss is a mainstay of gardens, and as much a part of a lawn as grass is in Europe and the US. Grown well, moss can bring a unique, calming, emerald-green cushion to walls and steps.

Care: 3/5

Effort: 2/5

Rebelliousness: 2/5

Plant division: Bryophyta

Max size: 1½in (4cm) tall, unlimited spread

Color: green

Flowers: n/a

Pot friendly: yes

Soil: any poorly drained, damp

Situation: full shade, part shade

Range: global (USDA zones unknown)

Origin: global

There are thousands of moss species. Common garden mosses in Europe include *Bryum capillare* (dark green with capsules) and *Brachythecium rutabulum* (light green and fluffy; left), *Polytrichastrum formosum* (with whorls of little leaves) and *Tortula muralis* (wall screw moss, opposite).

Moss is an ancient plant, closely related to ferns. It reproduces by spores, often released in variously shaped growths that are held above the main plant. It doesn't have a vascular system (which most plants do) to carry water around its structure, which restricts its height and means it needs constant moisture. Mosses are more like short straws that draw a little water up and aren't able to store it.

In the right conditions mosses create a soft matt of tight foliage unlike any other plant. A gardener can use them to add age, giving walls an air of "shabby chic" antiquity. But equally, it is possible to grow moss in ways that are contemporary and exciting. Moss draws the eye and hand: it is relaxing and mysterious to look at and enjoyably tactile.

Bringing moss into your garden

Unless you spend a lot of time researching the world of mosses in detail to find species suitable for your garden, the best approach is to provide the right conditions and wait. It's easiest to grow lots of moss in areas of high humidity, such as on the coast. Work with the types of moss already growing naturally in your area, as these are most likely to thrive in your garden. Moss will always find its way to shady, damp areas of walls and steps and our job is to leave it to grow rather than to scrape it off. Even if it dies back in summer, the chances are it will come right back in rainier fall.

Moss needs a wall in full shade that—one way or other (from a hose or rainwater)—remains damp all year round. This is unlikely to be the external wall of a house where damp is a problem, and more likely to be a garden wall that draws moisture upward, or the retaining wall of a raised bed. A shady seating area tucked away in a corner would be perfect. The best environments for moss are almost always north-facing, away from burning sun. (*Tortula muralis*, wall screw moss, is perhaps an exception, forming little tufts on the tops of walls from fall to spring before retreating back in the heat of summer.)

Contemporary uses include allowing moss to run wild, creating as large a sheet as possible. The dream would be an entire, perfectly green wall of it. It can have incredible impact, especially when it grows vertically or along the rises of steps. Once you have moss growing en masse, you can think about shaping it, carefully scraping it into contemporary squares, zigzags, or circles as a living graffiti.

In traditional gardens it's fun to let moss grow wherever it wants—don't be tempted to remove little spots of it too early as these can grow into more substantial vertical clumps. Try using moss to make a garden quickly look established and lived in, leaving it to grow up bird baths and statues, as well as walls.

Tropical or foliage gardens always benefit from having some moss, which adds variety to the textures and lush greenery. Once you have enough moss, you can be particularly adventurous, using it as a substrate in its own right—try growing plants such as ferns (see p.148) in it for a truly prehistoric look.

Invasiveness

Moss is really a problem only in extremely wet or humid areas and, even then, you'd have to leave it to its own devices for a long time for it to cause trouble. Roofs and guttering are the obvious problem areas, but a quick clean once a year is enough to keep moss in check.

If you happen to find moss growing rampantly through your garden, count yourself lucky to have the right conditions (most of us don't), and encourage it to create that wonderful sheet of soft, tactile emerald green.

Control

Scrape off surfaces with a paint scraper or firm scrubbing brush. Remove as much "substrate" (that is, soil) from wall surfaces so that the moss can't grow back. Most importantly, look for ways to remove dampness in structures, as moss can't grow on dry surfaces.

Cultivated varieties

Cultivars do exist in Japan, but otherwise are very hard to come by.

Yuko Nagamura — Landscape designer, TabbyCat Landscapes

Designer and head gardener, who grew up in Japan around Japanese gardens before training in western-style plant design, working on multiple award-winning gardens around the world.

How important are gardens to Japanese society? Sadly, the Japanese traditional garden is totally undervalued. Culturally, it's in decline, with preserved gardens tending only to be tourist attractions. There are no reasons to keep the Japanese garden when it is only a cost and no value when selling a property. Japan has the world's most expensive land price and inheritance tax. Also, the lifestyle of average Japanese people is time-poor and the Japanese garden is a very low priority. However, we can be hopeful that society still has the image of a garden as a place for relaxing or having healthy, quality time. There is slowly a growing interest in naturalistic gardens, vertical greening, and roof gardens.

Do you think attitudes toward garden weeds are different in Japan compared with other countries, or are they the same? Traditional Japanese gardens limit plant palettes and are strict on weeding, just like European formal gardens. But it's harder work because what we see as a "weed" is much more invasive and vigorous in our climate. Our humid summer makes weeding overwhelming.

Are any weeds considered beautiful and could they be included in garden designs with some planning? Some plants, like *Galium*, were never seen as a garden plant or meadow flower here. When I asked a nursery to pick it from the roadside and propagate it for me, they had never had such a crazy request. Sometimes New Perennial Movement designs include *Calamagrostis brachytricha*, *Imperata cylindrica*, *Solidago* spp., *Panicum*, *Molinia* …. I hesitate to use those as ornamental plants in Japan, because they can be too invasive to appreciate.

What are the worst weeds in Japanese gardens? *Miscanthus sinensis*, *Cayratia japonica*, *Artemisia indica* var. *maximowiczii*, *Imperata cylindrica*, *Poa annua*, *Digitaria ciliaris*, *Equisetum arvense* (see p.27), *Houttuynia cordata*, *Solidago canadensis* var. *scabra*, and *Euphorbia supina*. Another Japanese weed, *Macleaya cordata*, may be beautiful to Western people's eyes, but it is a completely vicious weed here. When I was a trainee gardener, John Brookes included *Macleaya cordata* in a planting palette for an English garden in Japan. Visitors were upset—they told me to pull it out otherwise they would demand a refund on their entrance fee.

Do you have any favorite weeds seen in Japanese gardens? Not sure whether it's a weed, but any seedling of trees, such as *Acer* seedlings, brought by bird droppings amuses me. They have a short life-span in a Japanese garden, but they are cute. In Western gardens in Japan, I sometimes leave *Paederia scandens*, *Oenothera speciosa*, *Corydalis* sp., *Spiranthes sinensis*, *Lilium formosanum*, and *Hemisteptia lyrata* to grow in planting beds, as lucky free additions.

How did the use of moss in Japanese gardens come about? We now have specialist moss nurseries and a certain market for moss sheets. Gardeners give intensive watering until the moss has settled. Even in Japanese gardens, some moss is a weed and removed. Moss has an aging effect and adds green color in shade and on rock. I think originally moss came with garden rocks, growing slowly if the new environment was suitable. *Leucobryum juniperoideum*, *Racomitrium canescens*, and *Hypnum plumaeforme* Wilson are favorite garden varieties.

Is moss easy to care for? Yes, if the garden is suitable for naturalizing it. No, if the moss needs regular care or irrigation. The warming climate is not helping: the heat one summer caused browning in a famous moss temple in Kyoto, and there is no cure for excess of heat and strong sunlight.

Some plants from Asia like *Fallopia japonica* and *Kudzu* are incredibly invasive weeds in Europe and the USA. What stops them from being so aggressive in their native habitat? Global warming may help for *Fallopia* matters. I grew up in the southwest of Japan and had never seen *Fallopia japonica* (see p.28) until I started studying in the UK. When I traveled to Hokkaido in northern Japan for the first time, I finally saw *Fallopia* on the roadside. So, I understand it is vigorous in cool weather. *Kudzu* (see p.32) runs wild here, too. In the old days, elderly people dug up the root and used it for starch. These days, everybody buys potato starch from supermarkets and so the plant goes wild. Although, traditional Japanese-style, confectionery makers still use *Kudzu* powder.

Chapter 9

Weeds for Big Spaces

Weeds aren't always tiny things growing between cracks in paving. Sometimes they can be the size of a car, if not bigger! Don't be scared by the thought of Weedzilla terrorizing your garden. With the right strategy, you can use these stately rogues to great and colorful effect.

Butterfly bush

Buddleja davidii

It's no wonder that *Buddleja davidii* has earned the common name, butterfly bush—beautiful, long, purple flower spikes bloom from mid-summer with gray-tinted leaves and the scent of honey, attracting the fluttering of butterflies.

Care: 0/5

Effort: 3/5

Rebelliousness: 4/5

☠

Plant family: Scrophulariaceae

Max size: 24 feet (8m) tall, 24 feet (8m) wide

Color: mauve, pink, purple, white

Flowers: June–September

Pot friendly: no

Soil: poor, slightly moist soil

Situation: full sun

Range: global (USDA hardiness zones 5–10)

Origin: China

A large number of shrubs and small trees flower in spring, which makes the later-flowering *Buddleja davidii* an invaluable garden plant and no doubt one of the reasons it was originally introduced as an ornamental.

Butterflies have to be factored into the look of *Buddleja davidii*, to ignore them is to do the plant an injustice.

Its habit is to grow in an arched fountain, with new shoots growing up to 6 feet (2m) in length through spring, before flowers appear at the tips. This fast growth makes it possible (and beneficial) to hard prune *Buddleja davidii* in winter, reducing its size to keep it compact. During this dormant period, usually toward the end of winter, cut all stems back to between 12in (30cm) and 23½in (60cm) from the ground, depending on how tall you want it to grow by summer. Always cut back to bud.

Although considered less weedy in the US, around the world—particularly Europe—*Buddleja davidii* is a real weed of waste areas. It enjoys environments that we create but no longer maintain—vacant spaces and abandoned buildings and walls. Its ability to re-nature areas, despite the harshest conditions, is admirable—in a nuclear explosion I suspect *Buddleja davidii* would join the cockroaches as survivors.

Bringing *Buddleja davidii* into your garden
When you spot seedlings—their leaves are the giveaway—you can easily dig them up and plant them in your garden. While not suitable for long-term pot life, you can grow them on in large pots for a year or two before planting. They flower from a young age.

Buddleja davidii's flower color, shape, and habit can vary quite wildly, especially in cities. Color is obvious with whites, pinks, and darker purples, but look closely at the shape of the flowers, too. Some are larger, others are fatter and fuller; some are bolt upright, others hanging. Occasionally, you'll spot differences in the way that they flower, some spikes holding a solid purple all over until finished, while most start flowering at one end, finishing at the tip. For this reason, like roses, it's best to take hardwood cuttings of 8–12in (20–30cm), as these will be genetic clones with the same attributes as the parent. Bury two-thirds of the sticks in the ground or in pots until they've rooted, then plant out.

Buddleja davidii makes a good standalone specimen in a lawn or meadow, as well as in part of a mixed garden bed. I often plant it at the back of designed beds, bringing a substantial splash of color that rises out of smaller perennials and annuals, just as many plants have stopped flowering. It grows in almost any soil, preferring free-draining soils in full sun.

It combines well with other silver-leaved plants, such as *Cynara cardunculus*, *Melianthus major*, *Artemisia*, and *Stachys byzantina*. *Salvia nemorosa*, which seems to pair with almost anything, makes a good companion to *Buddleja davidii* thanks to its similar coloring, as does *Verbena bonariensis*. *Echinacea purpurea* in pink or "White Swan," steely blue *Echinops bannaticus*, and purple *Monarda* "Scorpion" make for good companions, too. Try growing *Lathyrus latifolius* (see p.160) through it for colorful pops of pink, alongside the softer mauve; or ornamental grasses, such as *Miscanthus sinensis* "Gracillimus," alongside it; or transparent *Stipa gigantea* in front.

Note that in some countries, and in some states in the US, there are strict regulations about planting *Buddleja davidii*, so please check.

Invasiveness
In normal gardens *Buddleja davidii* is not invasive. It gently self-seeds, but not excessively—the few seedlings are obvious and easily yanked out. It's unmanaged vacant spaces that are the problem, as the occasional offspring thrive. Take steps to prevent your *Buddleja davidii* escaping into the wild.

Control
It's simple when small: just pull out the seedlings by hand, removing the weak root systems as you do so. If you prune your *Buddleja davidii* to keep it small, consider spending ten minutes each summer using secateurs or pruners to deadhead the spent flowers before they can set seed. For larger shrubs that need removing, cut to the ground and then dig out the root system completely. This can be a big job.

Cultivated varieties
There are hundreds of cultivars of *Buddleja davidii*, including dark purple "Black Knight," magenta "Royal Red," "White Profusion," and new dwarf varieties intended for pots, including "Tutti Frutti." In addition, many more *Buddleja* species exist, including the orange-flowered *Buddleja globosa* and weeping *Buddleja alternifolia*.

Broad-leaved everlasting sweet pea

Lathyrus latifolius

Imagine a problem-free sweet pea that keeps going all summer long and returns again next year .... Well, imagine no more, because weedy *Lathyrus latifolius* has obtained its name for good reason. It is a beautiful and vigorous plant with all the looks and charm of a traditional garden sweet pea.

Care: 0/5

Effort: 3/5

Rebelliousness: 4/5

Plant family: Fabaceae

Max size: 9 feet (3m) tall, 9 feet (3m) wide

Color: magenta

Flowers: June–September

Pot friendly: yes

Soil: poor and slightly moist

Situation: full sun

Range: global (USDA hardiness zones 5–9)

Origin: Europe, northern Africa

Lathyrus latifolius has large, bright pink flowers that grow in dense clusters and keep flowering all summer. To me, the fact that it runs rampant is ideal, and more than makes up for the fact that it has no fragrance (which may be a dealbreaker for some). It can be used as a cut flower, too.

On very hot, sunny days you can hear the ripe seed pods cracking open as they twist, causing them to explode under the pressure, firing seeds everywhere. In the wild *Lathyrus latifolius* loves growing in the middle of meadows, forming mounds among the grass and other wildflowers. In a garden meadow, then, it will bring sweeps of bright color.

Bringing *Lathyrus latifolius* into your garden
My plant self-seeded in the middle of my community garden, so I dug up a large chunk of root and planted it in the garden. The plant forms a deep taproot that can be hard to dig out without damage. However, it also produces rhizomes—spreading roots below the soil that bring new shoots—which can be cut off once they've formed their own roots and shoots. Alternatively, collect seeds from the brown, crispy pods in mid–late summer.

Grow the plant up a pergola, obelisk, fence, or wall. Its scale means that it grows large and dense without losing the beauty of the flowers. You can even grow it over shrubs and small trees that can cope with its romping. For example, grow it through a yew hedge—a tough plant able to cope with shade. The daring among us can grow it in a large garden if you're prepared for the plants to mingle and compete for attention. In rows or over low fences, it will form a bright pink hedge. Better yet, pair it with a white or purple (or both) *Clematis viticella*, allowing these vigorous climbers to battle it out while you admire the floral fireworks.

As a perennial, *Lathyrus latifolius* will come back each spring— just cut to the ground in winter. I've grown it in a 13½ × 13½in (35 × 35cm) pot on my sunny patio, meaning it would also survive on a balcony in full sun, too.

Invasiveness
There's nothing sweet about this pea: it's big and brutish, spreading as far as it can. Self-seeding readily (its seeds are heavy and will drop quickly to the ground), and spreading from rhizomes, one plant can quickly form a clump. Beware: its beauty will easily dazzle you until it's too late and things are out of hand. That said, it spreads gradually from the parent plant rather than quickly overtaking an entire garden.

Control
Pull out rhizomes when you spot them and snip off seed pods as they form. Alternatively, grow the plant in large pots on a patio, where it

can't spread, or sink a plant into the ground to stop the spread of the roots as you would mint. Other barriers, such as Butyl pond liner (see p.43), work well, too, although make sure water can run out of the bottom of the lining as the plant doesn't like soil that is too wet. Keep a watchful eye for its obvious seedlings and pull them out or hoe them while young.

Cultivated varieties
"White Pearl" is pure white; "Rosa Pearle" is light pink.

Staghorn sumach

Rhus typhina

Rhus typhina is a shrub with multiple stems that grow in a quirky, highly sculptural way. Leaves are long and divided into smaller leaflets. They look exotic or tropical and give this weedy, moderately rebellious shrub a contemporary and stylish feel.

Care: 0/5

Effort: 3/5

Rebelliousness: 3/5

Plant family: Anacardiaceae

Max size: 15 feet (5m) tall, 15 feet (5m) wide

Color: green, white, red

Flowers: July–August

Pot friendly: yes

Soil: any

Situation: full sun, part shade

Range: global (USDA hardiness zones 3–8)

Origin: eastern North America

I first spotted *Rhus typhina* growing randomly in front gardens having self-seeded. The combination of the stems, which look like twisted bonsai, with the palm-tree-like leaves makes for a unique, eye-catching plant. While *Rhus thyphina* does have some basic flowers in summer, it's fall when this plant excels, providing a multi-colored display of red, orange, and yellow leaves that eventually will fall. Spikes of fluffy seed heads appear at the same time and last into fall on the bare stems. Even without leaves, those sculptural stems add real interest to a garden. The common name staghorn sumach is because the downy stems look similar to the antlers of a stag.

Bringing *Rhus typhina* into your garden

You can buy this plant as an ornamental, or keep an eye out for rooted seedlings. Dig up and transplant the seedlings into your garden in spring or fall. In fall, you can collect (or buy) seeds, which you should sow in spring. The plant will grow in any soil and it prefers things on the drier side, in full sun, and will even grow in large pots. It will thrive in sunny, modern courtyards.

Design-wise it works well at the back of flowering garden beds and in shrub gardens. It looks particularly good as a focal point in meadows, prairies, and lawns. Its palm-like leaves mean it suits tropical gardens and, thanks to its size, it's perfect for growing in small gardens. Remove the lower leaves to enhance the effect of it looking like a tree.

Planting near other fall- and winter-interest plants can be really effective. The red of the *Rhus typhina* seed heads complementing red rose hips and other berries, such as those on *Pyracantha*. Among acers or cherry trees or near a *Ginkgo biloba*, the plant's fall leaf can be very dramatic. As *Rhus typhina* is deciduous, try underplanting with *Hellebores* and winter-flowering bulbs, such as *Galanthus*.

Invasiveness

Native to eastern US, *Rhus typhina* is a vigorus plant that will produce rhizomatous roots that make shoots around the parent plant. It also self-seeds easily, explaining why you will often find it growing randomly in unkempt gardens or empty lots as a weed around the world.

Control

Dig up the seedlings as soon as you see them and rip out shoots you don't want around the parent plant. Coppice it by cutting to the ground to keep its size in check—new shoots will form from the base. You can stop its spread by burying a Butyl pond-liner barrier (see p.43) into the ground around the plant as you would for bamboo.

Cultivated varieties

"Tiger Eyes" has sharply toothed, lime-green leaves, and a low-growing habit; while "Dissecta" has finely divided leaves.

Dog rose

Rosa canina

Rosa canina, and all wild roses, with their simple, wildlife-friendly flowers, are contemporary and stylish—a rebellious breath of pure air in an otherwise cluttered market of blowsiness.

Care: 2/5	
Effort: 3/5	
Rebelliousness: 3/5	
☠	

Plant family: Rosaceae	
Max size: 12 feet (4m) tall, 12 feet (4m)	
Color: white to pink	
Flowers: June	
Pot friendly: no	
Soil: any	
Situation: full sun	
Range: global (USDA hardiness zones 3–7)	
Origin: Europe, northern Africa, western Asia	

Rosa canina is a vigorous shrub with long, arching stems covered in thorns. It's deciduous, but in the summer is covered in attractive leaves that generally don't attract the same diseases as garden roses. The main event is a single flush of flowers in early summer. Masses of white or light pink flowers, loved by bees, are simple with a single row of petals around yellow stamen. This is followed by bright red rosehips in fall, which birds love. In the home the hips are often used in fall cut-flower arrangements.

Did you know?
Rosa canina has edible petals. Try drying them to make a calming tea. Or use them to infuse gin or vodka. Alternatively, you can just add the petals to your bath for a decadent soak.

You can eat the hips, too—their high vitamin-C content made them a popular snack in Europe during the World Wars. They also make a nutritious tea: boil them up for about ten minutes and then strain.

Bringing *Rosa canina* into your garden
There are a number of rebellious wild rose species. It's best to grow the one you like the look of most. *Rosa canina*'s flower color can vary in the wild with some plants being pink, others white, and some in-between.

The best way to grow your own is to take a cutting in fall for an exact clone of the parent plant. When the plant has lost its leaves and is dormant, cut a long length of stem, at least 23½–39½in (60–100cm) long. Cut this again into pieces about 8in (20cm) long, making sure you cut at a 45-degree angle just above a leaf bud at the top (the angle sheds rainwater and reminds you which way is up!). Cut flat at the bottom.

Either bury the cut stems in the ground in a sheltered spot or in a pot with two-thirds below the soil or compost (angled end upward). Put the pots in a sheltered spot or into a greenhouse and water frequently. In spring you should be rewarded with leaves telling you the pieces of stem have rooted.

Alternatively, you can buy from suppliers—as hedging they're inexpensive plants.

The plant's simplicity helps *Rosa canina* fit into modern gardens where the traditional or formal look of fuller roses can jar. Its looser nature looks perfect alongside meadow and prairie plantings. A white *Rosa canina* looks very smart near other pure white flowers, such as *Astrantia major* "Shaggy" or *Digitalis purpurea* f. *albiflora* (see p.21).

Unlike many garden roses, *Rosa canina* doesn't need much—if any—pruning. Remove old or damaged stems at the base. Over time, if

the plant becomes overcrowded or leggy, cut out a few stems (again, down at the base), which will prompt new shoots to grow lower down. Don't remove all of the stems in one go, though, because the plant flowers on the previous year's wood.

Invasiveness
Rosa canina is vigorous and needs space, growing to 9–12 feet (3–4m) over time. However, it's not particularly invasive, producing offspring slowly. In the wild it spreads seeds from its hips as its main means of propagation. The hips will drop to the floor—where birds will often eat them and spread the seeds. It is considered a noxious weedin Calforina, Hawaii, Oregon, and Washington.

Control
It's pointless trying to stop the spread of seeds from an established plant, so the main means of control is to keep an eye open for seedlings and to pull them out when you spot them. Make sure to remove the roots, otherwise the plant will grow back. Similarly, if you're digging out an established plant, ensure the roots come with it.

Cultivated varieties
There are cultivated varieties that tend to be hybrids with other roses and lose the purity of the species' simple flowers. In the wild there are a number of widespread species and hybrids making it hard to tell them apart. *Rosa arvensis* is slightly smaller than *Rosa canina*, while *Rosa rugosa*, from eastern Asia, has large, dark magenta flowers (and is more invasive).

Gorse

Ulex europaeus

Few things look or smell as beautiful as a hillside smothered in the bright yellow flowers of *Ulex europaeus* in spring. Often you can smell its coconut–almond fragrance before you see the brilliance of the glowing golden flowers.

Care: 0/5

Effort: 3/5

Rebelliousness: 3/5

Plant family: Fabaceae

Max size: 9 feet (3m) tall, 9 feet (3m) wide

Color: yellow

Flowers: April–June

Pot friendly: no

Soil: poor, slightly moist soil

Situation: full sun

Range: global (USDA zones unknown)

Origin: Europe

Ulex europaeus is regarded around the world as a dazzling spectacle—its flowers are the easy sell. Mainly found on the west and east coasts forming irregular humps, young plants fire out shoots in every direction. These grow to different lengths and develop their own lateral shoots. The result is arrow-shaped branches at all angles, which sounds chaotic on paper, but in real life these form a beautiful and dense sculptural shape. Eventually, when mature, each branch develops into a small hummock that wouldn't look out of place in a modern art gallery. The plant's leaves have evolved into pale gray–green, viciously sharp spines.

Did you know?
A handful of freshly picked *Ulex europaeus* petals added to a bottle of gin with a few tablespoons of sugar to taste and left in a dark place will, after a few weeks of daily shaking, form a sweet gin that tastes just as the flowers smell.

Bringing *Ulex europaeus* into your garden
A couple of months after flowering, in mid-summer you'll spot little brown seed pods. Once these have started cracking open, they're ready to collect. Sow the seeds into pots or the ground. Young plants have little round leaves at first, not spines (which appear later). If you spot small seedlings growing, you can dig these up and transplant them. The plant prefers an acid or neutral soil that drains well in full sun.

The shape of *Ulex europaeus* works perfectly alongside naturalistic plantings, particularly near annual and perennial meadows, where the froth of planting is both contrasted with the density of the shrub and mirrored by its loose form. Grow it at the back of garden beds knowing that there will be yellow flowers in spring, matching with *Narcissus* and *Forsythia* or contrasting with *Tulipa* or *Allium*.

Its glaucous foliage throughout summer and winter combines well with the whites of plants such as *Leucanthemum maxima* or the silvers and purples of *Cynara cardunculus* (the leaf form contrasting in texture, too). Alternatively, try it as a backdrop to the strongly vertical grasses *Molinia* "Transparent" and *Sorghastrum nutans*. Of course, the foliage will work well alongside other yellows, too, such as the flowers of *Rudbeckia* and *Helianthus*.

Used as a hedge, gorse creates an unusual, light green, informal boundary with the bonus of not only flowers in spring, but a near impenetrable security barrier!

Invasiveness
I can't decide if *Ulex europaeus* is invasive or simply hard to get rid of—probably both. When the dry pods explode, seeds are catapulted from the plant. In correct conditions these will germinate and grow into

new shrubs. Open or low grassy areas have little competition from other shrubs allowing *Ulex europaeus* to spread. In small and urban gardens there's really no risk of a mass invasion, because there is less chance for the seeds to germinate thanks to paving and other plants.

Control
Burning *Ulex europaeus* is one of the only practical ways to control established sweeps of it. Obviously, seek permission first: unsurprisingly, in most countries, using a gardening flame gun comes with a number of legal requirements and you need to be totally sure the fire will not spread.

Hoe any seedlings, and use shears or call a professional with a chainsaw to make light work of an overgrown shrub, making sure you dig out all of the roots.

Cultivated varieties
"Flore Pleno" has double flowers, while "Aureus" has petals of different shades.

Rod Randall — Biologist and Invasive Plants Expert, Government of Western Australia

Leading authority on weeds around the world, who has been instrumental in controlling invasive weeds in Australia, now working to inform regulation.

Are there any plants that people in Australia consider garden weeds that you think are actually quite beautiful and easy to grow? I quite like *Oxalis*, including the relatively common *Oxalis purpurea*: stunning pink flowers with a yellow throat popping out of a dense, matted layer of dark green clover-shaped leaves. *Oxalis flava* is also a favorite—stunning yellow flowers. *Oxalis* species in general are rather hated here; they are just too rampant for most people, too much work to keep in check. However, in the 1920s an old, now deceased, friend was given a paper bag full of *Oxalis* bulbs by his teacher for being an outstanding student and he planted them in his mother's garden. The house was levelled in an earthquake in the 1960s and the family ploughed in the garden to extend an adjoining paddock. The *Oxalis pes-caprae* bulbs survived and continue to thrive to this day. These are tough plants, I've seen them coming up through meters of rubble!

Is there one weed that you particularly like the look of? *Zaluzianskya divaricata*—a tiny little thing with a stunning flower. Most people are rather disdainful, but I like it and it pops up in the most unlikely places.

Can native weeds even be beneficial to gardens, such as for wildlife and blocking out other unwanted weeds? Sure, most certainly—although in a garden any plant could be considered a weed. In Australia native species in gardens fulfil important functions as food and shelter for native birds and the smaller marsupials. We have bandicoots, also called quendas, living in and around our gardens in my outer metro suburb and they like dense growth that they can hide under to avoid getting picked off by the foxes and cats. We also have many small nectivorous birds and heaps of parrots that all thrive on native garden plants, so I really can't begrudge any native if it gets a little rampant, as the locals do enjoy the side benefits.

How can people grow plants that happily spread around while preventing them from taking over? That's just called gardening, isn't it? It's what my mother spends all day doing most days—pruning, trimming, pulling out plants where they aren't wanted or when they grow over other, more desired plants.

We have a native creeper called *Hardenbergia comptoniana* that goes feral around here.

Are there things gardeners can do to control and prevent weeds spreading into the wild? Composting. Proper composting. Running your cuttings and trimmings through a shredder helps, as does ensuring the compost is well rotted before using it. Otherwise many councils will accept garden waste and compost it for use on local projects. That's far better than dumping garden waste in the bush, which is a major source of local weed problems. I also use a crushed gravel as mulch and spread it deep (2–4in/5–10cm). It never breaks down, maintains the soil moisture over summer and is pretty decent at keeping weed seedlings at bay.

What are the worst weeds that Australian gardeners should avoid? *Hedera helix* (p.132) is a monster. Another that bothers many people is *Vinca major*. I've spoken to people in tears on the phone who cannot control this beast. *Schinus terebinthifolius* is another that people often regret planting once they disturb its roots and it suckers into dense clumps.

Is there a balance or new approach people should take with regard to gardening that's more mindful of the environment while still producing attractive, interesting spaces? Sure, avoid planting environmental weeds. That is, avoid planting those species that locally are impacting on the native biodiversity. For example, plants that produce copious amounts of seed that are spread by birds can have a huge impact on the surrounding environment. Plants like *Cotoneaster* species and even grapes—they can be weedy here. In Western Australia we have a garden plant called *Asparagus asparagoides*, which is a significant environmental weed that spreads easily out of gardens via bird poop. Twenty years ago no one really knew about environmental weeds, it was something ecologists and biologists knew about but it wasn't mainstream. These days it's easy to determine what your local environmental weeds are. My preference is to not plant them. But, at the very least ensuring they never set seed or spread beyond a firmly defined and defended limit is always a good start.

Glossary

Annual: a plant that grows, sets seed and dies in one year.

Biennial: a plant that grows leaves in the first year and then flowers, sets seed and dies the second year.

Binomial: the botanical name of a plant, made up of both the Genus (e.g. *Bellis*) and a specific epithet (e.g. *perennis*) which, when used together, form the species (e.g. *Bellis perennis*).

Bulb: fleshy underground leaves that protect a new stem and store food for the plant.

Bulbils: secondary bulbs that grow from the parent, forming new plants.

Cultivars: plants that do not appear naturally in the wild, bred by people.

Deciduous: a plant that sheds leaves annually (usually during extremes of weather, e.g. winter).

Evergreen: a plant that keeps its leaves all year round.

Family: a botanical grouping of plants with related characteristics (sitting above Genus and usually containing multiple genera).

Fertile: soil with a high nutrient value usually derived from humus (rotten organic matter such as leaf debris or rotten manure).

Fibrous: many very thin roots, often densely packed.

Gametophyte: fascinating sexual phase in the life cycle of some plants such as ferns.

Genus: a botanical grouping of plant species with closely related characteristics (sitting beneath Family and above Species).

Germination: when the right conditions trigger a seed to start growing out of dormancy.

Herbaceous: a plant that has no woody stem, often but not always dying back once a year.

Hybrid: the offspring of two plants with different characteristics, sometimes from different species.

Lobe: the rounded or pointed part of a leaf.

Mulch: a thin layer of a substance (e.g. compost, bark chip) spread over the top of soil to lock in moisture, suppress weeds and often add nutrients.

Nectary: an organ in some flowers that produces nectar specifically to attract pollinators.

Nodules: growths on roots of leguminous plants (e.g. clover, peas) that store nitrogen from the air.

Ornamental: a decorative plant, i.e. not planted for food or other practical purpose.

Perennial: living for multiple years.

Petiole: leaf stalk.

Propagate: to breed plants.

Ray: a tiny flower that has evolved into what looks like a showy petal to attract pollinators (usually seen on flowers in the daisy/ *Asteraceae* family).

Rhizomes: roots that spread horizontally underground, developing new shoots along them.

Rootstock: the base and roots of a plant.

Runner: see Stolon.

Sap: a liquid transporting nutrients around plants.

Seedling: a baby plant grown from seed.

Shrub: a woody, usually multi-stemmed perennial, smaller than a tree.

Species (sp.): a group of plants with distinct characteristics that can breed with one another (sitting beneath Genus).

Spore: a microscopic organism produced by some plants instead of seeds that grow into new plants (other organisms like fungi also produce spores).

Sporophyte: the spore-producing stage of some plants, e.g. ferns we know are the sporophyte stage of their life-cycle.

Sterile: unable to reproduce.

Stolons: above-ground shoots that usually grow horizontally with roots and shoots growing along them creating new plants. Also called Runners.

Subspecies (ssp.): plants in a species that are geographically isolated enough to have naturally evolved slightly different or unique characteristics.

Substrate: soil, compost, or other plant-growing media.

Taproot: a single large dominant root (e.g. a carrot).

Tuber: thickened part of a stem or Rhizome found underground (e.g. potatoes, dahlias).

Variety (var.): plants in a species with naturally occurring differences (e.g. rounded vs elongated leaves).

Further Reading and Useful Websites

Books

Planting in a Post-Wild World: Designing Plant Communities for Resilient Landscapes by Claudia West and Thomas Rainer (2015, Timber Press).

Practical Herbs 1 & 2 by Henriette Kress (2011 and 2013, Yrtit ja Yrttiterapia).

RHS Encyclopedia of Gardening by Christopher Brickell (3rd edition, 2007, Dorling Kindersley).

The Book of Weeds: How to Deal with Plants that Behave Badly by Kenneth Thompson (2009, Dorling Kindersley).

The Weed Forager's Handbook: A Guide to Edible and Medicinal Weeds in Australia by Adam Grubb and Annie Raser-Rowland (2012, Hyland House Publishing).

Weeds: An Organic, Earth-friendly Guide to Their Identification, Use and Control by John Walker (2nd edition 2016, Earth Friendly Books).

Weeds: Friend or Foe? by Sally Roth (2002, Reader's Digest).

Weeds of North America by Richard Dickinson and France Royer (2014, University of Chicago Press).

Weeds: The Story of Outlaw Plants by Richard Mabey (2010, Profile Books Ltd.).

Weeds, Weeding (& Darwin) by William Edmonds (2013, Frances Lincoln).

Wild Flowers of Britain and Ireland by Marjorie Blamey, Richard Fitter, and Alastair Fitter (2nd edition, 2013, Bloomsbury Natural History).

Wild Flowers of the Mediterranean: A Complete Guide to the Islands and Coastal Regions by Christopher Grey-Wilson and Marjorie Blamey (2004, A&C Black).

Wonderful Weeds by Madeline Harley (2016, Papadakis).

Websites

"A Global Compendium of Weeds" by Rod P. Randall (3rd edition, 2017): cabi.org/isc/FullTextPDF/2017/20173071957.pdf.

Royal Horticultural Society: rhs.org.uk.

American Horticultural Society: ahsgardening.org.

Center for Invasive Species and Ecosystem Health weed database: invasive.org.

List of Invasive Alien Species of (European) Union concern: ec.europa.eu/environment/nature/invasivealien/list/index_en.htm.

"The Introduced Flora of Australia and its Weed Status" by Rod P. Randall: trove.nla.gov.au/work/11184831?selectedversion=NBD43424386.

Buy weeds and seeds

Nowhere sells listed "weed seeds" but you often find them online under the labels of "wildflower" and "meadow plant."

Native plants are easiest to find:

Australia
nativeshop.com.au
wildseedaustralia.com.au

Mainland Europe
wildflowerseeds.eu

North America
americanmeadows.com
wildflowermix.com

UK
meadowmania.co.uk
naturescape.co.uk
seedaholic.com
wildflower.co.uk
wildflowers.uk
wildflowershop.co.uk

More Weeds to Consider

Additional weeds by category

For colorful, sunny gardens
Achillea millefolium, common yarrow
Bituminaria bituminosa
Centranthus ruber, Jupiter's beard (p.120)
Centaurea nigra, common knapweed
　　(p.80)
Centaurea scabiosa, greater knapweed
Dipsacus fullonum, common teasel (p.66)
Eschscholzia californica, Californian
　　poppy (p.68)
Euphorbia helioscopia, sun spurge
Lathyrus latifolius, broad-leaved everlasting
　　sweet pea (p.160)
Leucanthemum vulgare, ox-eye daisy (p.84)
Lythrum salicaria, purple loosestrife (p.108)
Malva neglecta, dwarf mallow
Oenothera biennis, common evening
　　primrose (p.72)
Papaver rhoeas, common poppy
Persicaria maculosa, redshank
Rosa spp. (*canina* p.164)
Solidago canadensis, Canadian goldenrod

For dry and poor soils
Achillea millefolium,
　　common yarrow
Aethusa cynapium, fool's parsley
Euphorbia helioscopia, sun spurge
Hypochaeris radicata, cat's ear (p.82)
Leucanthemum vulgare, ox-eye daisy (p.84)
Malva neglecta, dwarf mallow
Matricaria discoidea, pineapple weed
Ranunculus bulbosus, bulbous buttercup
Solidago canadensis,
　　Canadian goldenrod
Verbascum thapsus, great mullein (p.23)
Zaluzianskya divaricata, spreading night flox

For meadows
Achillea millefolium, common yarrow
Anthemis arvensis, corn chamomile
Cirsium vulgare, spear thistle
Glebionis segetum, corn marigold
Matricaria chamomilla, German chamomile
Papaver rhoeas, common poppy
Pilosella aurantiaca, orange hawkweed
　　(p.124)
Pilosella officinarum, mouse-ear hawkweed
Prunella vulgaris, selfheal
Plantago lanceolata, ribwort plantain
Potentilla anserina, silverweed
Taraxacum officinale, dandelion

For shady gardens
Allium ursinum, wild garlic
Arum maculatum, lords-and-ladies
Campanula rapunculoides,
　　creeping bellflower
Convolvulus arvensis, field bindweed
Digitalis purpurea, foxglove (p.21)
Galium odoratum, sweet woodruff
Hyacinthoides non-scripta, English
　　bluebells (p.22)
Hylotelephium telephium, orpine
Lamium purpureum, red deadnettle
Melica uniflora, wood melic
Prunella vulgaris, selfheal
Silene dioica, red campion
Symphytum officinale, common comfrey

For rich, damp soils
Cirsium vulgare, spear thistle
Juncus communis, candle rush
Prunella vulgaris, selfheal

For containers, pots, and window boxes
Achillea millefolium, common yarrow
Daucus carota, Queen Anne's Lace (p.54)
Melica uniflora, wood melic
Oxalis spp., sorrel
Rhus typhina, staghorn sumach
　　(large pot) (p.162)

For ground cover
Lysimachia nummularia, creeping Jenny
Petasites fragrans, winter heliotrope
Tussilago farfara, coltsfoot

For steps and walls
Saxifraga spp.
Umbilicus rupestris, navel wort

Climbers and shrubs
Cytisus scoparius, common broom
Clematis vitalba, old man's beard
Fallopia baldschuanica, Russian vine
Lonicera japonica, Japanese
    honeysuckle
Phytolocca americana, poke weed
Solanum dulcamara,
    woody nightshade

Edible and nutritious weeds
Many weeds are edible but only eat those you are 100% sure are safe. Some beneficial weeds to try include:

Aegopodium podagraria, ground elder (p.25)
    In spring its new shoots can be fried
    and eaten.
Allium ursinum, wild garlic—its leaves can
    be eaten raw and added to meals as

you would with chives. The flowers
    are edible too.
Chenopodium album, fat hen—
    can be eaten raw or cooked like
    spinach, and the flower shoots
    can be used like broccoli. Very
    high in vitamins and other healthy
    nutrients.
Equisetum arvense, field horsetail (p.27)—
    once dried, use as a silica-rich tea for
    healthy bones.
Potentilla anserina, silverweed—the skinny
    roots can be cooked and eaten like
    nutty parsnips.
Primula vulgaris, primrose (p.23)—flowers
    can be eaten raw.
Rubus fruticosus, European blackberry (p.33)
    —blackberries can be eaten raw or
    cooked and are rich in Vitamin E and
    other nutrients.
Stellaria media, chick weed—can be eaten
    raw in salad or used to make a pesto.
    Rich in Vitamin C.
Taraxacum officinale, dandelion—the whole
    plant is edible. The young leaves can be
    eaten like lettuce and flowers can
    be fried.
Trifolium pratense, red clover (p.88)—the

flowers can be eaten raw and taste
    slightly sweet.
Umbilicus rupestris, navelwort—leaves can
    be eaten raw, tasting like peas.
Urtica dioica, stinging nettle—leaves can be
    eaten cooked and are very nutrient-
    dense. Great for teas and soup.

Weeds as cut flowers
It's worth experimenting with weeds as cut flowers and foliage. Some that last well in a vase include:

Achillea millefolium, common yarrow
Anthriscus sylvestris, wild chervil (p.104)
Centaurea nigra, common knapweed (p.80)
Centaurea scabiosa, greater knapweed
Daucus carota, Queen Anne's Lace (p.54)
Dipsacus fullonum, common teasel (p.66)
Leucanthemum vulgare, ox-eye daisy (p.84)
Persicaria maculosa, redshank
Pteridium aquilinum, bracken (for foliage)
Rosa spp. (flowers and hips) (*canina* p.164)

Index

Picture Credits

Caitlin Atkinson:
30 (left): Terremoto Landscape Architecture.

Jonathan Buckley:
58, **66** (Christopher Lloyd/Great Dixter), **75** (Carol Klein/Glebe Cottage), **104** (National Trust/Hidcote), **107**, **117** (above and below), **129**, **142**, **143**, **148**, **158**, **160**, **165**, **166**.

Carol Casselden:
18, **25** (right), **32** (right), **67**, **72**, **85**, **86**, **97**, **100**, **101**, **111** (above), **120**, **141**, **147**. (All photographed at Great Dixter except **25**, **32** and **147**).

Britt Willoughby Dyer:
4, **8** (Bryan's Ground), **22** (right), **23** (left), **24**, **31**, **33**, **34**, **40** (both Bryan's Ground), **42**, **45**, **53**, **73**, **92**, **123** (both Nic Howard, RHS Chelsea Flower Show), **132**, **133**, **145**, **167**.

Jim Powell:
6–7, **16** (both Sarah Price, RHS Chelsea Flower Show), **28** (right), **38**, **41** (Mark Gregory, RHS Chelsea Flower Show), **56**, **60**, **61** (below), **68**, **74**, **84** (Jo Thompson, RHS Chatsworth Flower Show), **88**, **93**, **95**, **103**, **111** (below), **112**, **113**, **115**, **118** (Peterham Nurseries), **122**, **124**, **125** (above), **134**, **135**, **137** (below), **146**, **152-3**, **163** (below).

Kate St John:
29 (right).

Jack Wallington:
15, **19**, **20**, **21** (left), **29** (left), **36**, **37**, **44**, **51**, **57** (above, below), **59** (above, below), **61** (above), **65**, **69** (above, below), **70**, **71**, **79**, **81** (all), **82**, **83**, **89**, **91**, **94**, **96**, **98**, **99**, **109** (above, below), **110** (Patrick de Nangle), **116**, **119**, **121** (above), **125** (below), **127**, **128**, **136** (Eden Community Garden, London), **137** (above), **149**, **157**, **159**, **161**, **163** (above), **164**.

Rachel Warne:
11, **48** (both Angus Wilson), **55**, **105**, **162** (Beth Chatto Gardens).

Kendra Wilson:
21 (right), **22** (left), **23** (right, Easton Walled Gardens), **25** (left), **28** (left), **80** (Easton Walled Gardens), **87**.

Alamy Stock Photo:
17 The Picture Art Collection; **26** (right) Fir Mamet; **27** Blickwinkel; **32** (left) Inga Spence; **46** Foto-zone; **52** Susanne Masters; **106** Hervé Lenain; **150** Chris Mattison; **151** Zoonar GmbH.

Gap Photos:
12 Abby Rex; **26** (left) BBC Magazines Ltd; **30** (right) Jonathan Buckley; **39** StockFood GmbH; **43** Suzie Gibbons; **54** Mark Bolton (Martyn Wilson, RHS Hampton Court Flower Show); **108**, David Dixon; **121** (below) Julia Boulton; **130** Gary Smith; **131** John Glover; **144** Matt Anker.

Portrait credits:
62 Nicola Stocken, **76** Mikhail Scheglov/Flower Jam, **138** Rob Cardillo, **154** Yuko Nagamura, **168** Rod Randall.

Acknowledgements

Thank you to everyone at Laurence King for being wild enough about weeds to publish this book. To Camilla Morton for first believing in the idea—never has a banana split felt so momentous! Alice Graham for your diligence in helping shape the book. My editors: Judy Barratt, Deborah Hercun, Melissa Danny and Blanche Craig for crafting and fine tuning every word and layout into this finished article. Thank you Katherine Montgomery, for your help and knowledge in updating this American version. Masumi Briozzo, thank you for making hundreds of pages of weeds look as stylish as they deserve.

Kendra Wilson, your enthusiasm and support on this project has been so wonderful, thank you for seeing the beauty of weeds too.

Claudia West, James Basson, Penny Snell, Rod Randall and Yuko Nagamura, it was an honor to include you and your expertise. Stephen Barney and Benny Hawksbee your way of gardening has been inspirational to me, thank you for inviting me into your world.

To my partner Christopher Anderson for having the wisdom and endless patience to let my inner rebel grow.

Finally, this book is dedicated to everyone who sees beauty in all forms of life.